ENDOR:

Joanna Adams' faith is contagious. Her pursuit of the divine supernatural is passionate and her revelation of God's Word is eye-opening. Joanna has penned these God-given words not by the theories of men, but rather through the inspiration and instruction of the Holy Spirit—which brings freedom and life! In her new book, you will gain biblical wisdom, glean from personal testimonies, and comprehend the power of God that is available to set you totally free. Read this book and receive the deliverance you need!

JOSHUA MILLS
International Evangelist
International Glory Ministries
London, Ontario/Palm Springs, California

Joanna Adams is incredibly anointed as a speaker, deliverance minister, and now as an author. Joanna clearly explains how doors can be opened to demonic powers operating in our lives, as well as how to apply the blood of Jesus to rid ourselves of them. I have never seen such power in a corporate deliverance setting than when Joanna came to our church. She spoke to a full crowd and prayed with power and authority for individuals to be free from demonic strongholds. All of heaven broke loose! We have invited her back regularly ever since. Now, you can read the truths she gained in the secret place and from her years of effective ministry in her book *Closing the Door to Demons*. Joanna's ministry has affected not only my life but the lives of my family. I highly esteem her as a friend, minister, and anointed woman of God.

PATRICIA BOOTSMA
Senior Associate Pastor
Catch the Fire, Toronto
Director, Catch the Fire House of Prayer

For eighteen years, I have watched Joanna grow from a young, dedicated student into a powerful woman of God who is being used mightily in international deliverance ministry. She is an anointed minister with incredible passion and heart. She is a woman of integrity and excellence who is fully dedicated to answering the call of God. I believe *Closing the Door to Demons* is yet another avenue where God will use Joanna to set the captives free. I am so thrilled that she has taken the step to publish this much-needed resource for the body of Christ.

DR. BILL SUDDUTH
Presiding Apostle and President
International Society of Deliverance Ministers
Founder, Righteous Acts Ministries, Inc.

Closing the Door to Demons will challenge your mindset and bring much-needed revelation to those struggling to live the life of freedom that Christ came to give. Complete liberty is possible, and this book shows you how!

RENÉ MCINTYRE
Founder, President, and Senior Pastor
Trumpet of Truth Christian Ministries

CLOSING THE
DOOR TO
DEMONS

PRISON BOO
P.O. BO
Sharpes, F

CLOSING THE

DOOR TO
DEMONS

DELIVERANCE
STRATEGIES TO
STAYING FREE

JOANN
ADAM

DESTINY IMAGE® PUBLISHERS, INC.
P.O. Box 310, Shippensburg, PA 17257-0310
"Promoting Inspired Lives."

This book and all other Destiny Image and Destiny Image Fiction books are available at Christian bookstores and distributors worldwide.

Rockwell

ifton

eign distributors, call 717-532-3040.

destinyimage.com.

5

ted in the U.S.A.

DEDICATION

I dedicate this book to the Lord. God, I pray that You would anoint and cover each page of this book so that everyone who reads it finds freedom in You.

ACKNOWLEDGMENTS

I could not have written this book alone, and I am very grateful to those who helped me make it a reality.

First and foremost, I thank my heavenly Father for encouraging me through various prophetic words that now was the time to write this book, and for bringing the right people into my life to help make it possible.

To my husband, Derek Adams—thank you for your support and for all the fantastic feedback and great ideas that you brought forth. Thank you for always being my biggest cheerleader and promoter. I love you very much and count it a privilege to walk this life together with you. The best is yet to come!

Thank you, Dr. Russ and Pastor Mave Moyer, for the support and love that you have shown me over the past eighteen years. You have given me many opportunities to grow as a minister. You are stellar examples of how to walk in love and integrity. I am grateful for the trust you have had in me and for the freedom you have given me to spread my wings and fly!

I say a very special thank you to Elisa Sorbara for tirelessly working alongside me to make this book become a reality. Thank you for your fantastic editing skills and for your patience with me. You are a spiritual daughter and I am so proud of you.

I thank my mom, Mary Distaulo, for her encouragement and support. Your words confirmed to me that I was on the right track, and that this book would be a very useful tool in the hands of Christians. You are a true teacher and a fantastic editor. Thank you, Mom.

I thank Joshua Mills, Bill Sudduth, René McIntyre, and Patricia Bootsma for their support and endorsement of my work.

Last, but not least, to my son, Malachi—thank you for being so generous with your time and for letting Mommy work on the book. You are an amazing little man of God who will do mighty things for Him. I am so proud of you! Love, Mommy.

CONTENTS

FOREWORD

What a pleasure it is to write the Foreword for Joanna's book, *Closing the Door to Demons*. Joanna Adams is an extremely able minister—a powerhouse for God. She is anointed and appointed to the ministry of deliverance and freedom for such a time as this. Joanna is, and has been, a spiritual daughter to my wife, Mave, and I for more than eighteen years. She has brought us much joy as we have watched her grow and become all that God intended her to be. To see her move in her spiritual giftings and ministry calling has been one of our greatest privileges.

In this excellent book, Joanna has very skillfully weaved practical information and application with testimonies—both from Scripture and real-life experience—to paint a beautiful picture of the delivering power of God for today!

Many argue and fuss over doctrine and theology. They ask why blood-bought Christians struggle with demonic influence and oppression. The truth is that demons do not want to be discovered operating in and through our lives. When they remain hidden, they can go about their devilish tasks unhindered. I believe demons are also busy operating through people in the realm of theology, encouraging them to argue and debate endlessly over whether or not a Christian can have a demon. Meanwhile, practical and effective ministers are busy setting the captives free, so they can walk out a successful and balanced Christian life—one that is unencumbered by the enemy.

The Bible tells us that God's people are destroyed because of a *"lack of knowledge"* (Hosea 4:6). Jesus answered His prophetic mandate in Isaiah 61:4 to set the captives free and heal the brokenhearted. He declared and walked out His call to freedom ministry. One third of Jesus' recorded ministry was deliverance. He imparted to and launched His disciples to minister out of this same freedom ministry mandate.

While naysayers continue to argue, many are still caught up in the bondage of fear and repetitive sins. Addicts, alcoholics, and those suffering from sexual addictions do not always automatically stop struggling when they receive Jesus. We know this is true because we have worked with many who needed personal deliverance ministry and inner healing to truly be free. They gave their hearts to the Lord and their spirits were set free, but their souls are another issue. This is the part of us that works out our salvation with fear and trembling. We must choose to actively pursue obedience in the process of sanctification while keeping a healthy fear of offending God through disobedience. Personal choice is big!

Christians believe that Jesus died so we might be healed. We have prayer lines. We have prayer calls. People even come and stand in proxy for one another. Ministers lay hands and call forth the healing power of God to set people free from physical infirmity and inner brokenness. Why would we neglect the ministry of deliverance?

Thank you, Joanna, for bringing freedom ministry—a ministry that is valid and valuable for today—to the forefront through your God-given revelation, your own experience, and the testimonies of others. May your wonderful book provoke many to pursue their own personal freedom. I pray that when people read this practical manual they will hear the call of God to pursue, pick up the mantle, and embrace the ministry of deliverance for themselves.

Thank you, Joanna, for the wonderful teaching and practical training revealed in *Closing the Door to Demons*.

With much love and blessing,

Dr. Russ Moyer, President
Eagle Worldwide Ministries

INTRODUCTION

MY PERSONAL FREEDOM EXPERIENCE

Do you feel like something is holding you back from experiencing your fullest destiny in God? Do you experience negative cycles of bondage to sin and wonder why you can't get victory? Are you bombarded with negative thoughts to the point where there is no peace in your mind? Do you feel like you are in the middle of a spiritual battle and don't know how to win?

If you answered yes to any of these questions, I want you to know that you are not alone! I myself had a checkmark beside each one of these questions. It wasn't until I received deliverance ministry that I was completely set free from my own cycles of sin, mental torment, and spiritual bondage.

My first experience with deliverance ministry was completely life changing. In 1996, at age 21, I became totally set on fire for God. My salvation experience was absolutely astounding. I answered an altar call while attending a church that was preaching the uncompromised Word of God. Even though I did not understand what the minister was talking about, I knew that I wanted what he had. In that moment, I ran up to the front and the minister laid hands on me.

Immediately, I was slain in the Spirit and fell to the floor.

My body began to convulse. It was as if I was vomiting but I wasn't. Each time I convulsed, I saw a different sin that I had committed. My life was playing back before my eyes like a movie. Images of the drugs I had taken, the times I was intoxicated, the men I had slept with—I was seeing it all. I did not realize it at the time, but as I was seeing each sin, I was repenting for it and God was delivering me, right there on the church floor.

> After that experience, I went from being a promiscuous partyer to a lovesick worshipper of God who took every opportunity to be in His presence.

After several minutes of this taking place, a beam of light hit me on the top of my head and filled my entire body. What felt like liquid love and acceptance filled my whole being. God, in His transformative power, had changed me. When I stood up, I was no longer the same person.

After that experience, I went from being a promiscuous partyer to a lovesick worshipper of God who took every opportunity to be in His presence. I wanted more of Him, and I wanted to dedicate all of my life to Him. I decided from that point forward, I was going to live a holy and pure life. As much as I was committed to living free from sin, there were still certain things that I struggled with. Three years into my salvation experience, I was still fighting secret sins from which I could not get free.

Even after serving Him for several years, I still did not understand what deliverance was. I also did not realize that I needed it. As my walk with God continued, I became increasingly ashamed and confused as to why I was not free. I would cry out to the Lord for Him to liberate me from falling back into the same old sinful patterns. As I called upon Him, I would feel a degree of freedom, but there was still a struggle going on inside me—one that was frustrating and hindering me from fully living for God in purity and holiness.

It was only after I experienced another form of deliverance ministry that I was completely set free from the spirits that had been keeping me in bondage to sin. I underwent a personal deliverance ministry session with Russ Moyer, who is the president of Eagle Worldwide Ministries. During the session, God delivered me from spirits that had been residing inside me and had been causing me to fall repeatedly back into sin. I will never forget that day.

The session began with me reading a series of prayers aloud; I repented and renounced my sins and also the sins of my generations. I must admit, I was extremely embarrassed reading the prayers because I was still in a place where I was actively struggling with these sins. Regardless, I pressed through the embarrassment and read them with fervency.

Once I completed the prayers, Russ began calling spirits off and out of me, commanding that they leave me in the name of Jesus. I cried for several hours; and when it was over, I felt like I had helium balloons inside of me. It was as if I floated out of the room that day—and from that moment forward, I no longer struggled with those repetitive sins. I was absolutely free! I was so dramatically impacted and the change in me was so noticeable, that I returned to Russ the following week with some family members, so they could receive deliverance ministry as well.

Prior to my ministry session, I had never even heard of deliverance. I was a Christian, yes, but I had never heard it taught in church and I had never seen anyone receive a form of freedom ministry like I had received that day. I could never have imagined that fiery, passionate Christians could have a demon spirit dwelling inside them.

> The measure of freedom I received during my deliverance session was completely transformative. My entire Christian walk was set ablaze from that point forward.

Looking back now, I can see that the measure of freedom I received during my deliverance session was completely transformative. My entire Christian walk was set ablaze from that point forward. I was now more passionate and zealous for the Lord than ever before. I no longer struggled with those habitual sins, and the connected guilt and shame were gone as well. I also began to think more clearly.

There was a new level of peace inside me and a new boldness of who I was in Christ. I did not realize it at the time, but God was also setting me free as a way of preparing me to help bring this same type of freedom to others. If I had not first received deliverance myself, I do not think that I would have been able to fully answer the call of God on my life.

> There was a new level of peace inside me and a new boldness of who I was in Christ. I did not realize it at the time, but God was also setting me free as a way of preparing me to help bring this same type of freedom to others.

In 2003, I graduated from the Brownsville Revival School of Ministry in Pensacola, Florida. There, I had the opportunity to train with Bill Sudduth, who was part of the school's faculty at the time. His position involved leading, training, and equipping students to move in deliverance ministry. Bill Sudduth is now the head of the International Society of Deliverance Ministers (ISDM), a coalition of deliverance ministers from across North America and around the world, originally founded by C. Peter Wagner.

I began my deliverance training with Bill while studying at Bible school. He and his wife became spiritual parents to me. They lovingly mentored me and poured so much into my life. After graduation, I came as a missionary to Ontario, Canada, to serve with Russ Moyer in his ministry, Eagle Worldwide Ministries. He began training and mentoring me in deliverance ministry as well as prophetic ministry.

I also had the opportunity to train and learn from Roger Miller, a powerful deliverance minister from Tennessee, USA. He would frequently visit Eagle Worldwide Ministries in Canada. I would sit in with him during personal ministry sessions and also in times of group deliverance. Each of these deliverance ministers had their own methods and tactics. By working alongside them, I was able to glean, learn, and then implement the skills, tools, and anointings required to operate in deliverance ministry myself.

I feel strongly in the importance of deliverance ministry—when done properly—simply because I have seen the fruit of it firsthand in my own life, and subsequently in the lives of others. My hope is that this book will help you better understand what deliverance is, what the benefits of it are, and the need for it within the body of Christ, so that you too can walk in total freedom and answer the high call of God on your life!

In no way, however, do I claim to be an expert on deliverance. This book is simply an introduction to the idea that a Christian may need deliverance. It is a collection of testimonies, Scriptures, strategies, revelations, and guidelines that have been helpful to me in my walk as a Christian and as a deliverance minister.

As helpful as these tools have been, I still rely heavily on the Holy Spirit to tell me what is required for deliverance in each particular situation. I also understand and exercise my authority in Christ. All these elements together have resulted in the privilege of ministering deliverance successfully to many individuals and in maintaining freedom in my own life.

My prayer is that as you read this book, the Holy Spirit will move upon you and speak to you personally about each element and how it applies to your Christian walk. May you be blessed, and may the Lord help you walk in freedom every single day!

CHAPTER 1

CAN A CHRISTIAN HAVE A DEMON?

Is the possiblity of a demon attacking a believer something that only happened in biblical times? Is it something that only occurred before Christ died on the cross? Do demons today only attack the unbeliever? Should we stay away from demons, letting them be, in order to protect ourselves from getting hurt? Do demons even still exist at all?

Many Christians today may ask these questions and more. While we do become new creations when we invite Jesus into our hearts, that does not necessarily mean that we instantaneously become free from every demon that had previously been attacking us—nor does that guarantee a demon will never bother us ever again.

In this chapter, we will explore and answer these very questions, using biblical truths and Scripture examples to assist with our exploration.

Can a Christian have a demon? Does every Christian need deliverance? I believe that the short answer is yes! While a Christian cannot be demon *possessed,* I believe a Christian can be demon *oppressed.* As mentioned in the Introduction of this book, I myself was a perfect example of this. Being demon oppressed essentially means that Christians can be influenced, affected, and tormented by demons, even though they are believers.

Why is it that some born-again believers, who love the Lord, struggle chronically with things like anger, anxiety, depression, addictions, sickness, fear, and worry? Christians are struggling because there are demonic spirits oppressing them. This is just a short list of problems that can have a demonic root.

> Why is it that some born-again believers, who love the Lord, struggle chronically with things like anger, anxiety, depression, addictions, sickness, fear, and worry?

You are a spirit who has a soul, which lives in a body. In that respect, there are three parts to you: spirit, soul, and body. When you become a Christian, your spirit is immediately transformed and born again—clean and pure with no demonic activity. At the same time, your soul and your body begin the process of sanctification—the process of being made holy. Even though the

Holy Spirit is also there, He can only be as active as your soul and body allow Him to be. Demon spirits had been affecting your soul and body prior to the Holy Spirit coming in.

Many times, these oppressive spirits will leave on their own upon a person's conversion, because they hate the anointing of the Holy Spirit and the blood of Jesus. They also hate when a person is involved in anointed praise and worship, so they may flee voluntarily then as well.

I also believe, however, that many of these demons remain entrenched within a Christian's soul and body until they are actively driven out. Satan uses his demons to carry out assignments against Christians, and some of them do not abandon their assignment unless they are forced to do so. This was certainly the case in my own life, and this is why I believe it is extremely important for born-again believers to undergo some form of deliverance ministry in order to truly be free and able to walk in the fullness of their God-ordained destinies.

If, as a Christian, you pray regularly and do everything within your power to live a victorious, godly life, yet you still have areas that you can't get victory in, then I believe you should explore the notion that you could be experiencing demonic oppression and that you may need deliverance ministry.

Remember that satan is a deceiver. He wants Christians to believe that demons cannot affect them, or he wants Christians to be afraid of them, unaware of the authority they have over demons. In the King James Version in Hosea 4:6, God says, *"My people are destroyed for lack of knowledge...."* That is exactly what satan wants to happen. An unawareness of the demonic realm and how it can affect a Christian is the tool that satan can use to keep us in a place of torment. It is for this very reason that I have written this book.

DEMONS AND OPPRESSION

Let's start by discussing the demons themselves. I believe that demons are essentially fallen angels. When satan was cast out of heaven, his angels went with him. We read about this occurrence in Revelation 12:7-9 (ESV):

> *Now war arose in heaven, Michael and his angels fighting against the dragon. And the dragon and his angels fought back, but he was defeated, and there was no longer any place for them in heaven. And the great dragon was thrown down, that ancient serpent, who is called the devil and satan, the deceiver of the whole world—he was thrown down to the earth, and his angels were thrown down with him.*

Satan is still roaming this earth. He is using his angels—what we know as demons—as his weapons to seek, kill, and destroy both the unbeliever and the believer alike. The difference is that believers have the authority in Christ to overcome him and his demons. They just need to be aware and knowledgeable about how to walk in this authority before they can exercise it successfully.

> Satan is still roaming this earth. He is using his angels—what we know as demons—as his weapons to seek, kill, and destroy both the unbeliever and the believer alike.

Before we discuss how to exercise our authority as believers, we will first explore several ways in which we can identify if we or someone we know is being tormented by a demonic spirit and therefore require deliverance. As a deliverance minister, some of the most common indicators of demonic oppression that I have seen include: emotional disturbances; mind and thought life disturbances; outbursts or uncontrolled use of the tongue; uncontrollable fits of anger or rage; addictions; recurring nightmares; diseases or physical afflictions; and involvement in false religions, the occult, or false doctrines.

Emotional Disturbances

While everyone can experience emotional disturbances from time to time, these experiences become an indicator of demonic oppression when such disturbances are reoccurring, persistent, unexplainable, inescapable, or uncontrollable. A common example could be if someone is experiencing unexplainable continuous crying and sorrow. That person may be under the attack of a spirit of depression. If someone experiences overall emotional instability—going back and forth from feeling very high to feeling very low—this is a clear indicator that the individual needs freedom.

Mind and Thought Life Disturbances

Again, while we all experience this to some degree throughout our lives, these disturbances in our mind and thought life become an indicator of demonic oppression when they prevent us from having peace in our minds, keep us from functioning or sleeping properly, or prevent us from dwelling on God or the things of the Spirit.

Outbursts or Uncontrolled Use of the Tongue

If a Christian is praising God one minute and then swearing or cursing the next minute, this is an indicator that demonic oppression may be present in his or her life.

Uncontrollable Fits of Anger or Rage

If a Christian experiences anger to the point where it is uncontrollable, or is continuously angry at everything and everyone, this could indicate demonic oppression. While a Christian may not necessarily be an outwardly violent person or act on these impulses, reoccurring feelings of anger can still indicate a need for freedom.

Addictions

A Christian who is struggling with addictions of any nature may need deliverance—especially if that Christian has a desire to break the addiction but has been unsuccessful in all attempts to do so. Addictions can come in many forms. Commonly recognized addictions can be to things such as nicotine, alcohol, drugs, pornography, caffeine, or food. Less commonly recognized addictions can be to things such as video games, escapism, movies, and the occult. Any habit or behavior that controls a person—or that a person uses to alleviate pain—can be considered an addiction.

> When Christians are tormented with bad dreams, or if they constantly experience dreams with ungodly themes such as excessive violence, perversion, or sexual impurity, this is an indicator that they require freedom.

Recurring Nightmares

When Christians are tormented with bad dreams, or if they constantly experience dreams with ungodly themes such as excessive violence, perversion, or sexual impurity, this is an indicator that they require freedom. For example, a person suffering with demonic oppression may wake up in fear, shaking or with night sweats, or may have a recurring nightmare or theme, such as being chased, being raped, or being killed. A spirit of Incubus or Succubus may sexually attack a person at night. This can be very disturbing and tormenting. All of these are indicators that freedom ministry is required.

Diseases or Physical Afflictions

Some illnesses and physical afflictions can be the result of a spiritual issue, such as a spirit of bitterness or a spirit of infirmity, as described in Luke 13:11-13 (ESV):

> *And behold, there was a woman who had a disabling spirit for eighteen years. She was bent over and could not fully straighten herself. When Jesus saw her, he called her over and said to her, "Woman, you are freed from your disability." And he laid his hands on her, and immediately she was made straight, and she glorified God.*

Involvement in False Religions, the Occult, or False Doctrines

Whether it was before salvation or afterward, if a Christian has been involved in, practiced, read, or been indoctrinated with any kind of false religion, idol worship, witchcraft, occultism, spiritualism, false doctrines, Masonry, or anything of the like, that Christian will likely require deliverance ministry in order to be set free from the demonic spirits connected with these ungodly practices.

Spirits connected usually include fear and terror, infirmities or unusual illnesses, breathing problems, allergies, sinus issues, rebellion, and anger. People who have been involved with false religions or the occult often feel blocked, disconnected, and hindered from understanding the Word of God. This is often due to false doctrines they have been exposed to. Ultimately, they can feel disconnected from God and have a hard time experiencing His love and acceptance.

> Christians may wonder why they struggle with one particular issue. They may blame themselves, get frustrated, or begin to believe that they are incapable of living a holy and completely consecrated life.

Often, Christians may wonder why they struggle with one particular issue. They may blame themselves, get frustrated, or begin to believe that they are incapable of living a holy and completely consecrated life. It is unfortunate when Christians feel this way, as often there is a demonic presence at play in their lives, causing them this difficulty. While we do have choices to make and a part to play in our own freedom, demonic oppression is very real and can cause Christians to slip up in their walk time and time again.

Yes, Christians can experience demonic attack; but the good news is that because we have been born again, we have all the necessary tools at our disposal to walk in the freedom that Christ died for us to have. Throughout this book, you will learn more about the different types of demonic oppression that a Christian may experience—and ways you can *receive your freedom,* and how you can *maintain that freedom* as you continue in your journey with the Lord.

CHAPTER 2

HOW DO DEMON SPIRITS ENTER?

How do demonic spirits enter a person to oppress someone in the first place? If a person has been born again, how is it possible for a demon to come into that individual? I believe there are several different ways spirits can enter—many of which can occur pre-salvation or even upon conception. Some of the most common ways in which demons can enter: generationally; environmentally; sin; unforgiveness; sexually; blood covenants; transference from others around us; inner vows and word curses; occult or satanic ritual involvement. Now let's look at each of these in more depth.

COMMON ENTRYWAYS

Generationally

Have you ever heard the phrase, "Like father, like son?" It's much more than just a saying. Spirits can transfer into a person right from the time of conception in the womb. That is why we can look at our family members and those in our generational line and see similarities between their sins. A spirit of alcoholism, for example, can be passed down through the generations. Grandpa was an alcoholic, Dad was an alcoholic, and now the son is an alcoholic. This is an all-too-common scenario in families today. Any kind of spirit can be passed down in this manner; but examples of other commonly encountered generational spirits include anger, bitterness, infirmity, sexual impurity, mental illness, and rejection.

> If a person has been born again, how is it possible for a demon to come into that individual?

Such generational transference can be the result of sin or the result of a curse, as outlined in Exodus 20:5-6 in the Easy-to-Read Version of the Bible:

> *Don't worship or serve idols of any kind, because I, the Lord, am your God. I hate my people worshiping other gods. **People who sin** against me become my enemies, and I will punish them. And **I will punish their children, their grandchildren, and even their great-grandchildren**. But I will be very kind to people who love me and*

obey my commands. I will be kind to their families for thousands of generations.

We are provided with another biblical example of generational curses in Exodus 34:7 (ESV): *"...visiting the iniquity of the fathers on the children and the children's children, to the third and fourth generation."*

The good news is that when Christ came, He redeemed us from generational curses. Galatians 3:13 (NKJV) says that *"Christ has redeemed us from the curse of the law, having become a curse for us (for it is written, 'Cursed is everyone who hangs on a tree')."* Now we, as Christians, need to apply that freedom and redemptive power to our lives. Nehemiah 9:2 (ESV) even gives us the pattern to receive freedom from these curses: *"And the Israelites separated themselves from all foreigners and stood and confessed their sins and the iniquities of their fathers."*

When our generations sin, those sins give satan a legal right to torment us. He is permitted by God to do so because of the curses that have been released through those sins. When we confess and repent for our sins and the sins of our ancestors, this breaks the power of the curse and removes the right satan previously had to torment us. We are now in a position where we can live free from this oppression.

> When we confess and repent for our sins and the sins of our ancestors, this breaks the power of the curse and removes the right satan previously had to torment us.

Environmentally

Demonic spirits can enter a person through the senses, including touch, sight, and sound. What a person sees and hears will affect the person. For example, if someone is listening to music filled with rage and anger, a door is opened for spirits connected with that music to enter into that individual through the person's ears. If someone is watching pornography, the spirits attached to the pornography, such as lust, perversion, and fantasy, can enter through the person's eyes.

I remember an instance where a male client came to me wanting freedom from his addiction to pornography. He shared with me that he enjoyed watching pornography that involved two females being together. This client was also concerned with new homosexual feelings arising within him. For the first time in his life, he was feeling attracted to other men. During his session, the Lord revealed to me that because he engaged in watching pornography that involved same-sex interaction, the spirit that was on what he was watching had entered him, resulting in him now feeling interested in men.

I believe Christians should exercise caution with regard to what movies or TV shows they watch, what books or doctrines they read, what music they listen to, and what video games they play. While not every secular thing carries demonic spirits, many do. Therefore, it is important that we ask for discernment from God to know what to avoid and to stay protected from any transference of spirits from our environment.

Not all "Christian" things are safe either. I'll never forget, years ago, there was a famous Christian artist who had a popular CD. Many Christians were raving about it and playing it continuously. Each time I heard it, however, something was not sitting well with my spirit. I didn't know why, but each time I heard his music, it bothered me to the point where I had to turn it off. Years later, I found out why this CD irritated me. The artist came out openly as a homosexual. I was discerning the spirits that were attached to his sin and these spirits were coming through his music.

Remember, the Bible tells us that in this day even the elect will be deceived (see Matthew 24:24). Therefore, it is so important that we ask for wisdom and discernment to know what is safe and suitable for us to engage in. There is no need to obsess or worry— if we ask, God will speak, and then all we have to do is listen and act accordingly.

Sin

When we sin, we are essentially opening the door to the devil and giving him permission to torment us. Every Christian sins, but the key is to repent quickly. If we do not repent quickly, or if we continue to sin without any repentance at all, we risk inviting spirits into us that will require deliverance ministry to remove. Examples of sins include alcoholism, drugs, pornography, cursing authority or leadership, gossiping, backbiting, dishonoring, experimentation with or involvement in false religions or the occult, and unforgiveness—just to name a few.

> We must forgive. It's not an option; it's a commandment.

Unforgiveness

Being unwilling to forgive, or holding resentment, can allow spirits to afflict a person. Unforgiveness can also block a person from receiving freedom in general. We must forgive. It's not an option; it's a commandment. Even when we do not think we can, we must tell God that we at least have the desire to, and then He will help us from there. Matthew 6:14-15 (ESV) says that *"if you forgive others their trespasses, your heavenly Father will also forgive you, but if you do not forgive others their trespasses, neither will your Father forgive your trespasses."*

We will explore unforgiveness in greater depth in a later chapter, as it plays a very large role in freedom ministry.

Sexually

Demonic spirits can transfer into a person through sexual acts, especially sex outside of marriage. When a person has intercourse or engages in sexual activity with someone outside of the protection of the marriage covenant, that person is open to a transference of spirits. This means that person is now at risk of receiving any demonic spirits that his or her sexual partner has.

I'll never forget the unfortunate testimony of a young woman who experienced this type of demonic transference. This woman was healthy and mentally stable. She had a good outlook on life and was an all-around positive person. She had never experienced any form of mental illness until she slept with a man who suffered terribly with that problem. Shortly after their sexual encounter, she began to experience the same horrific mental symptoms as her lover. Because she sinned and had engaged with him sexually, she had now inherited his demonic spirits.

Unfortunately, this woman—like so many people today—had no understanding of transference and the spiritual dangers of having sex outside of the marriage covenant. I believe this is one reason the devil is constantly working to encourage promiscuity in the world today. Satan understands that if he can get people to engage in sex outside of marriage, he can gain an open door to oppress them. First Corinthians 6:15-20 (NKJV) says:

> *Do you not know that your bodies are members of Christ? Shall I then take the members of Christ and make them members of a harlot? Certainly not! Or do you not know that he who is joined to a harlot is one body with her? For "the two," He says, "shall become one flesh." But he who is joined to the Lord is one spirit with Him. Flee sexual immorality. Every sin that a man does is outside the body, but he who commits sexual immorality sins against his own body. Or do you not know that your body is the temple of the Holy Spirit who is in you, whom you have from God, and you are not your own? For you were bought with a price; therefore glorify God in your body and in your spirit, which are God's.*

Demonic spirits can be transferred through any ungodly sexual act, not just fornication. They can also be transferred through things like molestation, impure touching, oral sex, acts of sodomy, and rape. Any sexual act that is not protected and permitted by God under the marriage covenant can result in demonic oppression for the participants. Even if it was unwilling participation, any person involved will likely require freedom ministry.

> Any sexual act that is not protected
> and permitted by God under the
> marriage covenant can result in demonic
> oppression for the participants.

Blood Covenants

Any time blood is mixed or exchanged between two individuals, a transference of spirits can occur. In the same way that ungodly sexual acts can cause the spirits of one person to transfer into another, so can the act of combining blood.

A common example of a blood covenant is when two people choose to become "blood buddies." This is when two people cause themselves to bleed and then press those two bleeding areas together, effectively exchanging blood. Another common example of a blood covenant is getting a tattoo. When a person gets a tattoo, blood is involved, and that person is essentially entering into a blood covenant with the tattoo artist performing the procedure. This puts the person receiving the tattoo at risk of receiving any spirits that the artist may be carrying. Blood covenants need to be broken and renounced so any transferred demonic spirits can be evicted.

Transference From Others Around Us

A transference of demonic spirits can happen when we come into contact with another person. Spirits can be transferred between people who share a living space or spend a lot of time together. They can also be transferred within a church or ministry. Just as we can receive a good and godly spiritual transference when a person prays and lays hands on us, we can also receive a negative transference if that person is demonically oppressed.

For this reason, it is so very important that you use wisdom when allowing someone to pray for you. Equally important is for leaders to use wisdom when allowing others to pray for members of their congregation. If someone on the prayer team is living in sin, those spirits can transfer to the person receiving prayer through the laying on of hands. The opposite is also true in that if you are praying for someone who has demonic oppression, those spirits can transfer onto you after praying for the person.

We cannot allow this possibility to put fear in us and prevent us from receiving prayer or praying for others. We just need to ask God for wisdom. If we feel strange after we have received or given prayer, we can simply exercise our authority in Jesus to remove any transferred spirits.

If you wish to learn more about the transference of spirits through the laying on of hands, you can read about it further in Leviticus 16:20-22, Second Chronicles 29:20-24, and Numbers 8:9-13.

Inner Vows and Word Curses

Ungodly inner vows are statements we say inside or come into agreement with that are not God's will. Examples of inner vows can include, "I'm never getting married" or, "I will never serve God." Whether we vowed these things before salvation or after, they still carry spiritual weight and can permit demonic spirits to carry out the manifestation of these ungodly vows. If we previously vowed to never get married but now we desire marriage, we need to break that vow in order for the demonic forces working against us to be removed from our lives.

Word curses are similar to vows. Word curses are negativities we have spoken and released over ourselves, that others have released over us, or that we have released over others. Satan knows the power of the spoken word. He will try to make us use words to curse ourselves and others because then he can torment us with spirits that will work to bring those negative spoken words to pass. We will also explore word curses, their power, and how to break them in a later chapter.

Even widely accepted things such as reading horoscopes or getting your fortune told are forms of engaging with the occult and can carry spiritual consequences.

Occult or Satanic Ritual Involvement

If a person, or someone in their former generations, has had any degree of involvement in the occult or witchcraft, that person will likely require deliverance. When we think of involvement with the occult, we usually think of things like casting spells or reading tarot cards. Yes, those practices are definitely invitations for spirits to enter, but even widely accepted things such as reading horoscopes or getting your fortune told are forms of engaging with the occult and can carry spiritual consequences.

Involvement with, association with, or participation in any false religions, false doctrines, cults, Freemasonry, or satanic rituals can also be a way spirits can enter a person. Any time a person has made a pact with satan, come into agreement with satan, made a vow to serve satan, been dedicated to satan, or anything of that nature—whether consensual or not—it is highly likely that deliverance ministry will be required.

Demonic spirits can also enter through related activities including yoga (where common positions are rooted in false religions and the act of worshipping false gods), certain scout and guide organizations (where ungodly vows may be required), and martial arts (which can be rooted in rage and anger, resulting in rebellion).

Being knowledgeable of how the demonic realm can affect Christians is not to scare us—it is to empower us!

If you know that you have been involved in one or more of the areas listed in this chapter, there is no need to fear. Instead, rejoice that, regardless of your past, Jesus can set you free!

> Being knowledgeable of how the demonic realm can affect Christians is not to scare us—it is to empower us!

As you continue reading, you will learn tools that you can use to apply Jesus' liberating power to your life and walk in freedom from demonic oppression, despite anything in which you or your past generations have participated.

CHAPTER 3

WHAT IS DELIVERANCE?

What exactly is deliverance and how does it apply to a Christian? Simply put, from a believer's perspective, *deliverance can be defined as actively evicting demonic spirits.* It is the process of removing a spirit and its effects, thereby freeing and liberating the person it was tormenting. Deliverance ministry is a frontline, end-time ministry that attacks the enemy directly. It is a form of hand-to-hand combat against satan and his demons.

Some Christians may have been very successful in walking holy since salvation, yet still experience emotional disturbances, reoccurring struggles with sin, or other negative issues on a regular basis. As discussed in the previous chapter, there are several ways a spirit can enter a person—many of which can be a result of something that our generations did or that we engaged in prior to salvation. That is why, as a general rule, I believe it is good practice for all Christians to receive some form of deliverance ministry.

Never be ashamed of recognizing the need for and pursuing deliverance ministry. I believe deliverance ministry should be embraced and done regularly, with integrity, within the safety of the church. I believe church leaders, especially those who are working in some form of ministry, must receive deliverance ministry for themselves. This is necessary simply because those in ministry are often targeted by the devil.

> Never be ashamed of recognizing the need for and pursuing deliverance ministry.

It is important to understand that salvation does not necessarily wipe our slate clean in the area of demonic oppression. Instead, salvation gives us the tools to access the freedom for which Jesus died. Just as we have a part to play in asking forgiveness for our sins—they are not automatically forgiven—we also have a part to play in walking out our freedom. Deliverance is active; and you will learn in this book that we have a responsibility for our own freedom.

Deliverance is like peeling the layers of an onion. It is not always immediate. Often it is more like a journey that requires various forms of ministry over time. You may receive freedom in a personal ministry session led by a pastor or a leader. Deliverance can also occur in a group setting where people are experiencing ministry all at the same time. It may come directly from God Himself, or when involved in anointed praise and worship. Every person and every situation is different. Overall, the important thing is to acknowledge the need for deliverance, and then be open to receive it.

> While you may not necessarily be called to work in deliverance ministry, if you are a Christian you are still called to set the captives free!

Receiving freedom from God is great. It will change your life. Not only will it change your life, it will put you in a position where you can be used by God to help set others free. While you may not necessarily be called to work in deliverance ministry, if you are a Christian you are still called to set the captives free! There are several Scriptures that talk about this:

The Spirit of the Lord God is upon me, because the Lord has anointed me to bring good news to the poor; he has sent me to bind up the broken-hearted, to proclaim liberty to the captives, and the opening of the prison to those who are bound; to proclaim the year of the Lord's favor, and the day of vengeance of our God; to comfort all who

*mourn; to grant to those who mourn in Zion—
to give them a beautiful headdress instead of
ashes, the oil of gladness instead of mourning,
the garment of praise instead of a faint spirit;
that they may be called oaks of righteousness,
the planting of the Lord, that he may be glorified*
(Isaiah 61:1-3 ESV).

*And he [Jesus] said to them, "Go into all the world
and proclaim the gospel to the whole creation.
Whoever believes and is baptized will be saved,
but whoever does not believe will be condemned.
And these signs will accompany those who
believe: in my name they will cast out demons;
they will speak in new tongues; they will pick up
serpents with their hands; and if they drink any
deadly poison, it will not hurt them; they will lay
their hands on the sick, and they will recover"*
(Mark 16:15-18 ESV).

Let's look at some examples of how deliverance was received by those in the Bible. Sometimes when we think of Jesus, we just think of the instances where He healed the sick or the fact that He came to provide us with eternal life. Those truths are, of course, absolutely wonderful, but it is important that we do not forget that He very actively performed deliverances while He was here on earth. Approximately one third of Jesus' recorded ministry was deliverance. The following are a few biblical accounts of Jesus performing deliverances:

> *And when they had come to the multitude, a man came to Him, kneeling down to Him and saying, "Lord, have mercy on my son, for he is an epileptic and suffers severely; for he often falls into the fire and often into the water. So I brought him to Your disciples, but they could not cure him." Then Jesus answered and said, "O faithless and perverse generation, how long shall I be with you? How long shall I bear with you? Bring him here to Me." And Jesus rebuked the demon, and it came out of him; and the child was cured from that very hour* (Matthew 17:14-18 NKJV).
>
> *And [Jesus] went throughout all Galilee, preaching in their synagogues and casting out demons* (Mark 1:39 ESV).
>
> *When evening had come, they brought to Him many who were demon-possessed. And He cast out the spirits with a word, and healed all who were sick* (Matthew 8:16 NKJV).
>
> *And behold, there was a woman who had had a ꞇbling spirit for eighteen years. She was bent ꞁer and could not fully straighten herself. When Jesus saw her, he called her over and said to her, "Woman you are freed from your disability." And he laid his hands on her, and immediately she*

was made straight, and she glorified God (Luke
13:11-13 ESV).

We may look at these accounts and think that
demonic oppression was only something that had to
be dealt with before Christ died on the cross. We know
that this is not true, because of the command that Jesus
gives to His followers after His resurrection regarding
what they must do to continue in His ministry (Mark
16:15-18).

A STUNNING DELIVERANCE

As a deliverance minister, I have had the honor and
privilege of witnessing many Christians being set free
from bondages that had tormented them for years. The
most intense, most powerful deliverance I have ever
witnessed happened to a young woman who had been
suffering with a spirit of infirmity for nine years, similar
to the spirit that Jesus cast out in Luke 13:11. In an earlier chapter, we discussed how some physical illnesses
can be the result of demonic oppression. In the situation
of this young woman's illness, that was exactly the case.

She had just started attending my church when I
noticed that she always came wearing bandages all
over her joints. When I spoke to her about these bandages, she explained that she wore them because she
had a physical condition where her joints would slide
out of place, partially dislocating. She told me that it

was actually a physiotherapist who put this bandage tape on her, and that having it on her body helped to keep her joints from moving around so much. Aside from her condition being a debilitating one, it was also a very painful one. Because of this, she was attending physiotherapy five times a week, as it was the only way she could temporarily reduce the pain caused by her condition.

> The most intense, most powerful deliverance I have ever witnessed happened to a young woman who had been suffering with a spirit of infirmity for nine years, similar to the spirit that Jesus cast out in Luke 13:11.

Because of these high pain levels, this young woman had to stop attending regular schooling and switch to an online program. She had to give up numerous activities that had previously brought her joy, including athletics and playing multiple musical instruments. She struggled holding a pen, opening doors, washing her hair, and lifting anything weighing more than two pounds. She could not even open a water bottle. Even the most basic activities of daily life were struggles for her because of this condition.

She went on to explain to me that she had been suffering with this condition for nine years. It started randomly, and there was no cure for what she had. There were no available surgeries either. The doctors had told her that the condition was permanent and irreversible and that she would be this way for the rest of her life. Now, as a result, she was just living each day doing what she could to keep her pain levels as low as possible.

I explained to her that what she had, seemed to me, like a spiritual issue. I recounted the story of the woman in the Bible and explained to her that often physical conditions can be the result of a spiritual root. She was open to receiving deliverance ministry; and when I began to minister to her, it quickly became very clear to us that her condition did indeed have a spiritual root.

She was a dancer, and at age 15, right before this illness began, she participated in a dance activity that involved using her body in a sexual way. She also gathered those around her, cousins and friends, to participate in it with her. From the world's perspective what she did was not unacceptable, she was actually dancing a mainstream routine to a song from a very popular musical.

From God's perspective, however, what she was doing was definitely a sin. Our bodies are temples of the Holy Spirit, and what we learned as we were ministering to her was that it was this very act that had opened the door for a spirit of infirmity to come in and destroy her body.

Immediately, once this was revealed, she repented for this sin and the spirit no longer had a legal right to stay in her body and cause her pain. We then went ahead and exercised the authority given to us by Christ, using the name of Jesus to command that spirit of infirmity to leave her. Even though the legal right had been broken, that spirit still did not want to go. Her body had been that spirit's home for nine years, and it did not want to be evicted. I'll never forget the struggle. It wanted my assistant and me to give up, but we refused. She was on the floor screaming because of the pain it was causing her. Part of me wanted to stop and call the ambulance, but I knew that if we just kept pressing through, this spirit was going to leave her—and that is exactly what happened.

> There was a moment when the atmosphere completely shifted, and I knew that it had left. She got up off the floor and began shouting that the pain was gone!

There was a moment when the atmosphere completely shifted, and I knew that it had left. She got up off the floor and began shouting that the pain was gone! All of heaven broke out in that room. Immediately, my assistant and I hit the floor in a prostrate position and began worshipping God, thanking Him for the miracle He had just performed. We cut off all her bandages, and she had no problems moving without them. I witnessed her deliverance happen right before my eyes.

It has been several years now, and she is still totally pain-free. Her life has been completely changed and restored. Her physical illness entirely disappeared through deliverance ministry. Thank You, Jesus!

Demonic spirits are very real and are operating in the world today. The good news is, just like in the case of this young woman, the name of Jesus still works to set the captives free. We cannot allow the enemy to keep us in a place of shame or even a place of denial over what we may be struggling with. Those kinds of feelings are tactics the enemy uses to try to prevent people from positioning themselves to receive freedom. Satan and the spirits he uses to torment may also try to stop an individual from going to church or receiving prayer for deliverance. Those spirits do not want to be evicted, so they try whatever they can to prevent that from happening.

It is important for Christians to know that this may occur. Knowledge is power. If we know in advance that this may happen, it becomes easier to over-come and position ourselves in a place where we can receive freedom.

RECEIVING DELIVERANCE

How can a Christian receive deliverance? There are so many ways freedom can come! There is no one specific formula by which to receive freedom or no one specific way it may look like or feel like. Every person is uniquely created by God, and He has a different journey of freedom for each of us.

Ultimately, deliverance comes from one Source—God. We must be careful never to chase a minister, or anyone for that matter, or see a person as the source of bringing forward deliverance in our lives. Only God can do that. Does He use anointed men and women of God? Absolutely; but be careful not to fall into idolatry of humans. It's important to stay open to receive deliverance in whichever manner and timeframe God wants.

> It's important to stay open to receive deliverance in whichever manner and timeframe God wants.

We receive freedom: upon salvation; in a personal ministry session; during altar ministry; in group deliverance sessions or conferences; in personal prayer time; and during times of anointed praise and worship. We will now explore individually these methods that God uses to set us free:

Deliverance Upon Salvation

There have been many instances where as soon as a person dedicates his or her life to God, He sets that person free from something that had been greatly tormenting. My husband is a perfect example of this. Upon giving his life to Christ, God instantly delivered him from a lifestyle of drug and alcohol addiction. God can bring deliverance instantly when we say yes to Him. Even so, it is still a good idea for Christians to press in deeper and receive further ministry following salvation, as there often remain other issues that need to be dealt with.

Deliverance in a Personal Ministry Session

In the ministry I am part of, we hold what are called "personal ministry sessions." These are, essentially, appointments where a person comes to receive ministry directly from a deliverance minister. The person is asked to read a series of repentance and renunciation prayers, thereby breaking any legal rights that the enemy had to torment the person. After that, the minister begins to call spirits off the person—casting them out and commanding them to leave in the name of Jesus. Different ministries may offer similar types of personal ministry sessions. Basically, it is a time of prayer and deliverance hand-tailored just for that individual.

I facilitate many personal ministry sessions myself on a regular basis. I have seen great fruit from this type of ministry. Even the spirits themselves know how effective this type of deliverance can be, as often they will put up a fight and try whatever they can to stop the person from coming to his or her scheduled appointment.

Many individuals to whom I have ministered have shared with me that they underwent a tremendous struggle before arriving for ministry.

It is not uncommon for me to hear stories of individuals who, leading up to the appointment, have suddenly felt sick, been tormented aggressively in their thought life, or even lost their way as they were driving to the appointment. God provides an amazing ability for individuals to persevere through these attacks, however, and the results following their personal ministry sessions are always incredible.

During these appointments, my assistant (never perform a personal deliverance session alone!) and I minister deliverance to one person at a time and we refer to each as a "client." When I begin a personal ministry session, I share with the client what he or she can expect during our time together. I explain what deliverance can look like and what types of manifestations may occur. I do this to put the client at ease, as sometimes clients can arrive nervous, uncomfortable, and uncertain.

Deliverance and its accompanying manifestations can be different for everyone. Sometimes clients will not feel a thing. Sometimes clients will feel the spirit resisting (causing pain in their bodies, fatigue, confusion, etc.), but that resistance will lift, and they will begin to feel peace instead. Sometimes clients will outwardly manifest in the form of a cough, blink, burp, cry, or yawn. Sometimes they will need to blow their nose. Sometimes they may even feel sick to their stomach and vomit.

> Deliverance and its accompanying manifestations can be different for everyone.

Believe it or not, all of these manifestations are actually normal. I have ministered to many clients, and outward manifestations like this happen often. Sometimes I myself will even manifest with yawning, burping, and a runny nose, especially if the person I am praying for does not manifest. I have learned to embrace the uniqueness of each individual's time of deliverance. Rather than try to understand it, I simply get out of the way and allow the Holy Spirit to lead each ministry session. Nothing fazes me or upsets me. I am okay with whatever God requires for the client to be set free.

After I have described what to expect, I ask the client to briefly highlight the key issues or reasons why he or she has chosen to come for ministry. I let the client know that everything shared with me is confidential. I do not let the client chat for too long, as I have learned that spirits can use excessive talking as a stall tactic to try and delay the time of ministry. Once I have heard the client's primary reasons for scheduling the appointment,

I then have the client read a series of prayers, similar to the ones found throughout this book. These prayers are for the client to repent and renounce his or her own sins and the sins of previous generations. The prayers also lead the client through a time of forgiveness.

Once the prayers are completed, I move into deliverance ministry. I ask the client to look into my eyes, if possible, as the eyes are the window to the soul and can reveal which spirits are afflicting a person. No two deliverance sessions are alike. I follow the leading of the Holy Spirit to ensure that I am ministering in a way that is meeting that individual's exact needs.

Following deliverance, I pray for an infilling, asking the Lord to heal any areas left voided now that the spirits have been evicted. Spirits can also have claws, and often they will scratch, tear, and pull at the person's insides in an attempt to hold on to that person as long as possible. Sometimes clients will even cough up blood as spirits are leaving them. This may be hard for you to read or to even comprehend, but remember, there is nothing too big for God to heal—and often that is exactly what we see Him do.

I have witnessed clients' bodies heal, bones heal, and blood heal. It is amazing what happens when we ask. This is why it is so important to pray for an infilling afterward. I also ask God to release inner healing by praying for God's oil and wine to fill the person's heart and heal his or her emotions.

After we have prayed for inner healing, I always end the session by releasing a prophetic word over the client. I hand out resources that outline the steps a person should take to maintain the freedom. I explain the importance of making life changes moving forward. Deliverance is not a quick fix. It is a process, and it is the client's responsibility to walk it out, which may include changing certain habits, ending certain relationships, or getting rid of certain possessions.

I give the client an opportunity to ask any questions and also get the client's feedback on the experience. We discuss the possibility of a future session, if necessary. Often personal ministry sessions are so intense that the client can only take so much at once and sometimes more than one session is necessary.

> Often personal ministry sessions are so intense that the client can only take so much at once and sometimes more than one session is necessary.

When the appointment has concluded and the client has left, my assistant and I will pray over ourselves and the room, commanding all spirits that were loosed to go. We command them not to transfer, remain, or retaliate. We take a moment to cover with the blood of Jesus our loved ones, our possessions, and everything

God has given us stewardship over. We ask God to seal everything good that happened during the session with the blood of Jesus. This type of personalized deliverance prayer from a minister, pastor, or leader is one way God can bring forth deliverance.

DISCLAIMER: If you are a pastor or minister and you are considering offering this type of personal, hand-tailored deliverance ministry, please ensure that you first receive adequate training in deliverance ministry. Operating in proper training and protocol is crucial for both your safety and the safety of those for whom you pray. Deliverance ministry must be done properly, decently, and with integrity. You can receive such training in various places, including through the ministry I am part of. See Appendix C for details.

Deliverance During Altar Ministry

God can quickly and completely deliver individuals when they receive prayer from someone at the altar—or anywhere for that matter! At our church, following each service we call a prayer team to come to the altar. This team prays for any individuals who wish to receive ministry. During this time, team members can command demonic spirits to leave the person they are praying for. When deliverance occurs in this type of setting, it is often quick and not as in-depth as other forms of deliverance ministry, but it can still be just as effective.

Deliverance in Group Deliverance Sessions or Conferences

This occurs when a pastor or a minister prays and performs deliverance over a full congregation of people at once. A minister may do this from the pulpit on a Sunday morning during a sermon. A minister may also do this at a specific deliverance conference. It is a very effective way for God to minister to many people all at once. Much freedom can and has come forth in this manner.

This is a type of ministry that I perform regularly myself, and I have seen great results come from it. If you are a pastor or a leader of a church and are interested in having this type of ministry for your congregation, see Appendix C for details about how you can arrange a conference or a time of group ministry.

Deliverance in Personal Prayer Time

God is our Deliverer, and He can set us free without using anyone else at all. I have an amazing personal testimony of this type of deliverance occurring in my own life.

When I conduct personal ministry sessions, I always ask aloud for the Lord to send ministering angels to help assist with the deliverance process. Once during my personal prayer time, while I was alone in the privacy of my own home, I asked God to heal me, deliver me, and set me free. After I asked Him, I heard God say so clearly that He was sending His ministering angels to help me right now—exactly what I say when I am helping clients!

> The angels came immediately. I felt their presence so strongly. Right there, in that moment, my mouth just opened up and I felt the angels pull spirits out of me.

The angels came immediately. I felt their presence so strongly. Right there, in that moment, my mouth just opened up and I felt the angels pull spirits out of me. It was an absolutely amazing experience, and I was so set free!

Deliverance During Times of Anointed Praise and Worship

The anointing on praise and worship can cause demon spirits to go away because they do not wish to stay in that atmosphere.

HAPPY, HEALTHY LIVES

Once we have been set free, we will live much happier lives and be healthier mentally, physically, and emotionally. We will also now be in a position where we can be used of God to help set others free. Jesus did the hard work for us. All we have to do is have a proper revelation of who we are in Christ and exercise that authority to command demons to leave in the name of Jesus. Remember, Mark 16:17 (ESV) says that *"these signs will accompany those who believe; in my name they will cast out demons...."*

Jesus wants us to do this. He wants to work through us to set His children free. He even told His disciples when He sent them out in Matthew 10:8 (NIV) to *"Heal the sick, raise the dead, cleanse those who have leprosy, drive out demons. Freely you have received; freely give."*

In Luke 10:19 (NKJV) Jesus tells us, *"Behold, I give you the authority to trample on serpents and scorpions, and over all the power of the enemy, and nothing shall by any means hurt you."* That being said, also heed His warning in Luke 10:20 (NKJV): *"Nevertheless do not rejoice in this, that the spirits are subject to you, but rather rejoice because your names are written in heaven."*

The following chapters outline practical steps you can take and apply in your life to obtain freedom—closing the door to demons.

CHAPTER 4

FORGIVENESS? I THOUGHT I DID THAT

I believe there is a dimension of freedom that will never happen in our lives until we choose to forgive. The Word of God says we must forgive others in order to be forgiven ourselves. Forgiveness is not an option—it is a command. There are several examples in the Bible where God outlines the importance of forgiveness:

> *For if you forgive others their trespasses, your heavenly Father will also forgive you, but if you do not forgive others their trespasses, neither will your Father forgive your trespasses* (Matthew 6:14-15 ESV).
>
> *Then Peter came to Jesus and asked, "Lord, how many times shall I forgive my brother or sister who sins against me? Up to seven times?" Jesus answered, "I tell you, not seven times, but seventy-seven times* (Matthew 18:21-22 NIV).

And when you stand praying, if you hold anything against anyone, forgive them, so that your Father in heaven may forgive you your sins (Mark 11:25 NIV).

Bear with each other and forgive one another if any of you has a grievance against someone. Forgive as the Lord forgave you (Colossians 3:13 NIV).

Be kind to one another, tenderhearted, forgiving one another, as God in Christ forgave you (Ephesians 4:32 ESV).

God is serious about His command to forgive. We need to come to a place where we understand that we have absolutely no right to hold unforgiveness. Everyone gets hurt and the pain those hurts cause is very real. There is no denying that pain—and God understands. The act of forgiving someone, however, is not an act of acknowledging that what the person did was okay. It is an act of releasing the person to God, not because the person deserves to be released, but because it is commanded in the Word of God. Just like we need forgiveness from our own sins, God expects us to extend that same grace to others and will not tolerate anything less.

> God is serious about His command to forgive. We need to come to a place where we understand that we have absolutely no right to hold unforgiveness.

Apart from it being a command, forgiveness is also necessary for freedom and deliverance to happen in our lives. If we do not forgive, we essentially tie God's hands and the devil gets a legal right to torment us. God makes this very clear in Matthew 18:34-35 (NKJV):

> *And his master was angry, and delivered him to the torturers until he should pay all that was due to him. So My heavenly Father also will do to you if each of you, from his heart, does not forgive his brother his trespasses.*

You might be saying to yourself right now, *What? God is going to give me over to the torturers? Not my God!* Often when we think of God, we don't think of Him as one who would allow torture to come to His children. God absolutely does not want us to be tortured, which is why He has provided us with a way to escape this snare of the devil—simply forgive.

What is torture? What exactly is satan permitted to do to Christians who choose not to forgive? Torture can be defined as extreme pain, anguish of body or mind, agony, or torment. How does satan carry out this torture and torment over people who hold unforgiveness? These torturers described in the Bible are demonic spirits that have been given a right to torment a person because of the sin of unforgiveness.

If we harbor unforgiveness, it becomes like a seed within us. The more we water that seed—the longer we hold unforgiveness—the more it begins to grow into a plant of bitterness. Bitterness is essentially unfulfilled revenge. Hebrews 12:14-15 (ESV) says:

Strive for peace with everyone, and for the holiness without which no one will see the Lord. See to it that no one fails to obtain the grace of God; that no "root of bitterness" springs up and causes trouble, and by it many become defiled.

Not only will bitterness defile you but it will also defile those around you. Have you ever been around a bitter person? It can be both challenging and hurtful.

> Not only will bitterness defile you but it will also defile those around you.

Often Christians do not realize the toxic effects that sin, particularly unforgiveness, can have on their physical bodies. It can feel very heavy, weighing us down and making us feel very sick. God describes this in Psalm 38:3-4 (ESV):

There is no soundness in my flesh because of your indignation; there is no health in my bones because of my sin. For my iniquities have gone over my head; like a heavy burden, they are too heavy for me.

A spirit of bitterness is one that can cause many problems such as anger, hurt, and rage. Bitterness can also manifest itself as a physical ailment such as arthritis or joint pain. If you struggle with either of these ailments, ask yourself, *Am I angry at anyone? Am I bitter?* Your first step to freedom is to forgive.

I was conducting a personal deliverance session once with a client who had been complaining about extreme stomach pain. He had been to several doctors and nobody had been able to determine the cause of his pain. As I began ministering to him, we discovered that he had been holding unforgiveness toward several individuals. In the session, he made the choice to forgive them and released each of their names aloud to God.

As he was doing this, my assistant saw in the spirit that every time he released a name and forgave that person, a pin came out of his stomach. Those pins were demonic spirits that had been inside his stomach, causing anguish and pain. When the session was finished, his stomach pain was completely gone. His act of obedience and forgiveness broke the right the devil had to torment him with pain. He was fully healed!

There are earthly consequences of sin, as well as requirements to receive liberation from these consequences. Forgiveness is a major key. Regardless of what has been done to us, we must follow Jesus' example, as described in Luke 23:34 (ESV): *"And Jesus said, 'Father, forgive them, for they know not what they do.'"* Jesus was more blameless than we have ever been, yet He was able to forgive. Forgiveness is a choice. If we ask God to help us forgive, He will do just that.

In the numerous ministry sessions that I've had the privilege of leading, I have found that unforgiveness will block a person's freedom. I have also noticed that unless the person truly forgives, the session is not fruitful, and liberation is not achieved. Many times, clients that have been deeply hurt read a forgiveness prayer, making the choice to forgive, and God is able to move. Often clients become unblocked instantly and begin to weep right there on the spot as liberation takes place.

> I have found that unforgiveness will block a person's freedom. I have also noticed that unless the person truly forgives, the session is not fruitful, and liberation is not achieved.

Do you want to make the choice to forgive right now? Are you ready to be unblocked, putting an end to all the torture and torment? Are you ready to untie God's hands, so that He can remove the pain and hurt that you have been carrying? Say this prayer aloud and allow God to move on your heart:

FORGIVENESS PRAYER

Lord, I have unforgiveness in my heart. I con]
that I have not always loved others. I have har-
bored resentment and bitterness, but I am coming
to You now to ask You to help me forgive those
who have hurt me. I want to forgive them from
my heart. I don't know if I can, but I make the
choice to do so. Help me to forgive them. Please
take away the pain, the hurt, the resentment,
and the bitterness. Lord, show me now the people
I need to forgive, so I can release them and be
released myself.

Pause, and let the Holy Spirit show you the names
or faces of people you need to forgive. They may be
living or dead. Take your time; and as the Lord shows
them to you, forgive them in your own words. If God
shows you individuals you feel you have already forgiven, forgive them again anyway. If God is bringing
them to your memory, it is likely because you still need
to forgive them.

CHAPTER 5

DID I SAY THAT? THERE'S POWER IN THE TONGUE

In a previous chapter, we briefly discussed inner vows and word curses and the way that demonic spirits can hinder a person through them. Whether inner vows or word curses took place before or after salvation, they still carry spiritual weight. Demonic spirits are waiting to carry out the manifestation of these ungodly curses and vows. We will now explore both of these in greater depth.

INNER VOWS

An ungodly inner vow is a self-oriented commitment made in response to a person, experience, or desire in life. For example, when we experience hurt during childhood, a common reaction is to employ an emotional self-defense by making an inner vow that we will never let ourselves be vulnerable in that way again.

> As hurt individuals, we make these inner vows, thereby putting up walls around our hearts. Our priority becomes self-protection.

As hurt individuals, we make these inner vows, thereby putting up walls around our hearts. Our priority becomes self-protection. These vows can block communication and intimacy, among other things. The following are some examples of different inner vows a person could make:

"I will never...

...let anyone love me."

...share what is mine."

...let you see who I am."

...tell a woman anything."

...let a man control me."

...allow anyone to touch me."

...marry anyone like my father/mother."

...have children."

...trust anyone again."

...fall in love."

The result of an inner vow can vary and often depends on what exactly was vowed. For example, if a person vowed to never get married, but now that person desires marriage, that person may struggle with obtaining a successful marriage due to demonic spirits working against this area of his or her life as a result of the vow. The vow needs to be broken in order for the connected spirits to be removed.

WORD CURSES

Word curses can be negativity that we have spoken and released over ourselves. They can also be what others have released over us, or what we have released over others. Word curses are sins; and without repentance, these curses will open a door to demonic torment. Satan knows the power of the spoken word, and he will try to work through us by making us use words to curse ourselves and others—because the words we say have power.

> We may think of a word curse as something that a witch or a warlock says and releases. While word curses can come in that form, more common word curses are disguised in simple, everyday phrases that we often release over ourselves.

We may think of a word curse as something that a witch or a warlock says and releases. While word curses can come in that form, more common word curses are disguised in simple, everyday phrases that we often release over ourselves, such as, "My back is killing me,"

"I'm going crazy," "My kids never listen to me" or, "My job will be the death of me."

All of these statements, whether true or not, become word curses when spoken aloud and are very much alive and active. Proverbs 18:21 (NIV) tells us that *"The tongue has the power of life and death, and those who love it will eat its fruit."* Whatever you speak is going to come forward in your life. You are your own prophet! When we say something like, "My back is killing me," for example, we can open a door in the spiritual realm and come into agreement with spirits of pain and torment, thereby inviting them to torture us to the point where we do indeed have increased back trouble!

Unfortunately, I witnessed something similar to this firsthand in my own life. My father died at the young age of 55 from a brain tumor. Prior to my father's passing, he was acting very strangely. He was constantly in a frustrated state and would repeatedly say, "Once I own a Jaguar car, I'll be happy and then I can die." The devil took those words, which had power, and used them against my father—because that is exactly what happened to him. He finally got a Jaguar, but in less than a year he was diagnosed with a massive brain tumor. He died within eight weeks of being diagnosed.

It was only after his death, during my own personal time with the Lord, that God revealed this to me. We really do carry the power of life and death within our tongues. I am very intentional about speaking life-giving words over myself and my family. I believe all Christians should be extremely careful as to the words we use, and we should work hard to bridle our tongues.

As you can see by what happened to my father, the words we say have the power to entrap us. Proverbs 6:2 (NKJV) says, *"You are snared by the words of your mouth...."* Once we speak words, whether positive or negative, they are living and active. When we speak negative words over ourselves, satan will take those words and use them against us, just like he did to my father. Our words can cause us to, quite literally, loose hell over ourselves.

> Satan wants us to use our words to advance his kingdom. God, on the other hand, wants us to use our words to advance His Kingdom. He wants us to declare blessings aloud, lift up others, and speak life.

Satan wants us to use our words to advance his kingdom. God, on the other hand, wants us to use our words to advance His Kingdom. He wants us to declare blessings aloud, lift up others, and speak life. God has given us a tremendous level of power and authority in our tongues, but with that comes a tremendous level of responsibility. The Bible warns us that there will be eternal consequences for the choices we make concerning our spoken words. Matthew 12:37 (NIV) says, *"For by your words you will be acquitted, and by your words you will be condemned."*

We are the ones who must choose whether to speak life or death—blessings or curses. Every time we speak, we are advancing somebody's kingdom. Let's make sure it is God's Kingdom and not satan's. For learning's sake, we are going to go a little deeper and explore what happens when we release words that align with each of those kingdoms. We will begin with the kingdom of darkness.

Speaking negatively and aligning with satan's plans for our lives can bring forth much oppression. This oppression can come in the form of defilement, destruction, entrapment, barrenness, depression, despair, strife, judgment, punishment, death, and even separation from God.

The Bible provides us with many examples of the consequences that can come when a person chooses to speak death:

> *With their mouths the godless destroy their neighbors...* (Proverbs 11:9 NIV).
>
> *...a harsh word stirs up anger* (Proverbs 15:1 NKJV).
>
> *The mouths of fools are their undoing, and their lips are a snare to their very lives* (Proverbs 18:7 NIV).

If someone curses their father or mother, their lamp will be snuffed out in pitch darkness (Proverbs 20:20 NIV).

But whoever disowns me before others, I will disown before my Father in heaven (Matthew 10:33 NIV).

But I [Jesus] tell you that everyone will have to give account on the day of judgment for every empty word they have spoken (Matthew 12:36 NIV).

What goes into someone's mouth does not defile them, but what comes out of their mouth, that is what defiles them (Matthew 15:11 NIV).

But shun profane and idle babblings, for they will increase to more ungodliness (2 Timothy 2:16 NKJV).

But avoid foolish and ignorant disputes, knowing that they generate strife (2 Timothy 2:23 NKJV).

And the tongue is a fire, a world of iniquity. The tongue is so set among our members that it defiles the whole body, and sets on fire the course of nature; and it is set on fire by hell (James 3:6 NKJV).

These are just a few Scripture examples of the darkness that can come forth from our words. Our tongues may be small in size, but they carry a great amount of power. Now let's examine what happens when we use our tongues to advance the Kingdom of Light.

> Our tongues may be small in size, but they carry a great amount of power.

When we speak life, we bring forth the wonderful possibilities of receiving blessings, fulfillment, joy, fruitfulness, provision, protection, triumph, knowledge, wisdom, honor, health, grace, and eternal life, among many other pleasing aspects of life. The Bible provides us with several examples of the effects of a person who chooses to speak life:

The mouth of the righteous is a well of life... (Proverbs 10:11 NKJV).

The mouth of the righteous brings forth wisdom... (Proverbs 10:31 NKJV).

From the fruit of their lips people are filled with good things... (Proverbs 12:14 NIV).

...the tongue of the wise promotes health (Proverbs 12:18 NKJV).

The truthful lip shall be established forever... (Proverbs 12:19 NKJV).

From the fruit of their lips people enjoy good things... (Proverbs 13:2 NIV).

Those who guard their lips preserve their lives... (Proverbs 13:3 NIV).

A person finds joy in giving an apt reply—and how good is a timely word! (Proverbs 15:23 NIV).

The hearts of the wise make their mouths prudent, and their lips promote instruction. Gracious words are like a honeycomb, sweet to the soul and healing to the bones (Proverbs 16:23-24 NIV).

Those who guard their mouths and their tongues keep themselves from calamity (Proverbs 21:23 NIV).

Whoever acknowledges me before others, I will also acknowledge before my Father in heaven (Matthew 10:32 NIV).

Whoever would love life and see good days must keep their tongue from evil and their lips from deceitful speech (1 Peter 3:10 NIV).

They triumphed over him by the blood of the Lamb and by the word of their testimony... (Revelation 12:11 NIV).

> The power of life and death that sits in the tongue is so important for every Christian to understand.

The power of life and death that sits in the tongue is so important for every Christian to understand. In relation to the spirit realm and deliverance, when word curses have been released over us, we need to break them in order to prevent or stop the demonic oppression that comes along with such words.

FOUR SIMPLE STEPS

How do you break the power of these word curses and inner vows? You can break them by following four simple steps: repent, renounce, break, and bless.

1. **Repent.** The first thing you must do is repent to God for the words that you have spoken that were responsible for loosing hell over your life. In addition to resulting in demonic oppression, making ungodly vows and speaking curses are also sinful acts. You need to repent for that sin and ask God to cover it with the blood of Jesus.

2. **Renounce.** You need to disavow any agreement with the demonic spirits that were permitted to torture you through those curses. You do this by renouncing any spirits that you invited into your life.

3. **Break.** Next you must break the curse and its effects. Audibly use the name of Jesus to break the power of any word curses or connected spirits that resulted from what you spoke.

4. **Bless.** Finally, you must speak life, bless, and declare the outcome you want to see. Speak aloud truths from the Bible that contradict the negative words and curses

you have spoken in the past. Speak
ings and positive declarations int
areas of your life that have been afｔ‿‿‿‿
by those curses.

> Speak blessings and positive declarations
> into the areas of your life that have
> been affected by those curses.

Next is an example of how to apply these four steps
to a word curse. We'll use the previous example of the
statement, "I'm going crazy." To break that word curse,
you could say the following:

1. **Repent.** "God, I'm sorry for saying that I'm
   going crazy. I repent. Please forgive me of
   this sin."

2. **Renounce.** "I renounce all spirits of mental
   illness, confusion, mind fog *(simply list
   any symptoms or spirits you feel may be
   connected to the word curse or vow)*, and
   any other demonic spirits that I may have
   allowed to torment me because of what
   I said."

3. **Break.** "In the name of Jesus, I break every
   curse of craziness and mental illness that
   I have spoken over myself. I cancel all
   connected and related demons and their

effects, and command them to leave me now in the name of Jesus."

4. **Bless.** "Second Timothy 1:7 says that God has not given me a spirit of fear but of power, love, and a sound mind. I loose the blessing of clear thought and a sound mind over myself. I declare that I am not going crazy. My mind is at peace and completely aligned with the will of God for my life."

By following these four simple steps, we can effectively break the power of ungodly inner vows and word curses and be free from their connected demonic spirits. It is that simple; and the more you follow the steps, the more natural they will become. This same type of formula can and should also be used when others speak word curses over you.

> Not only do our own words have power over our lives, but the words that others speak over us do as well.

Not only do our own words have power over our lives, but the words that others speak over us do as well. This is why it is so important to surround yourself with people who are supportive of you, understand your walk with God, and are knowledgeable about the power of the tongue and the importance of speaking life not death.

If you know that God has called you to walk with or associate with individuals who speak curses over you, instead of rejecting them or becoming a hermit all together, just use wisdom. Make sure you are not speaking any curses along with them. Follow these steps to break the power of the curses they speak. If you do this, you will stop the spirits connected to their word curses from affecting your life.

CHAPTER 6

WHAT CAN BLOCK MY FREEDOM?

Satan is a legalist. If there is an avenue or a hook that he can use to block your freedom, he is going to use it to do exactly that. Satan has been given power over this earth, at least for the time being, and he uses that power to hinder Christians. He knows when he has a legal right to torment a person, and he will exercise it until it has been removed.

What exactly does the term "legal right" refer to in this case? Essentially, it means that satan is permitted by God to use demonic spirits to torment a person because of something that person or his or her generations did. In situations where satan has a legal right, God's hands are, in essence, tied, and He cannot help us until we repent. Instead, God will make us aware of any legal rights the enemy has to torment us. Once we are made aware, it is essential that we repent and renounce those sins. These are the tools and steps He provides us with to break satan's hold on us.

So far in this book, we have discussed three different ways freedom can be blocked: 1) unforgiveness; 2) ungodly vows, and 3) word curses. We have discussed what can cause those blockages and how to deal with them.

There are additional things, however, that may restrict a Christian's freedom, including: generational curses and iniquities; soul ties; witchcraft curses; unrepented sin; judgments; and a Leviathan spirit. We examine those next, explaining what they are and how to break their power.

GENERATIONAL CURSES AND INIQUITIES

As we discussed earlier, one way that spirits can enter a person is through his or her generational line. The sins of our ancestors can result in demonic spirits and curses being passed along to us. Remember, God tells us this in Exodus 34:7 (NKJV): *"...visiting the iniquity of the fathers upon the children and the children's children, to the third and fourth generation."*

When Christ came, He redeemed us from all generational curses. To apply this freedom to our lives, we need to confess the sins of our generations and repent, thereby breaking the hold the enemy had over us because of these sins. We may not know what our generations did specifically, but that is okay because God knows. We can still work with Him to receive our freedom. He does not want us to suffer from the effects of our ancestors' sins.

> We may not know what our generations did specifically, but that is okay because God knows. We can still work with Him to receive our freedom. He does not want us to suffer from the effects of our ancestors' sins.

My grandfather was involved in Masonry, which is a form of the occult. I was unaware of his involvement until I went to Bible school. During my schooling, there was a time when I was in my bedroom reading Bill Sudduth's book, *So Free*. As I was reading, I came to a part that talked about involvement in the Masonic Lodge. I had never personally been involved in any Masonic Lodges, but as I was reading this chapter I suddenly began choking and coughing. I began to receive deliverance from spirits connected with Masonry right there in my bedroom!

As I was experiencing deliverance, I began to have visions. I saw a picture of my grandparents' house. It was a scene from when I was a child. I was sitting at their kitchen table and my grandpa went into his closet and pulled out a red fez hat. Red fez hats are what the

wear. Shriners are connected to Masons. In
on, God was showing me that my grandfather
was a Mason, and he had opened the door for the curses
and spirits connected with Masonry to come into my
life. I remember being so set free and dramatically
impacted that I quickly got on the phone and called Bill
and Janet Sudduth.

Bill Sudduth not only wrote the book I had been
reading at the time, but he and his wife, Janet, were
also my mentors at the Brownsville Revival School of
Ministry where I was attending Bible school. They both
began to pray with me over the phone, and I received
even more freedom. Often, we do not even realize what
our generations have done, and as a result we are still
living with the effects of their sins.

Pray this prayer, believing that God will remove
the spirits that have been oppressing you because of
generational sins:

Breaking Generational Curses Prayer

Dear heavenly Father,

*I confess that I and my generations have sinned
against You. I am sorry for these sins and on
behalf of me and my generations, I repent and ask
for Your forgiveness.* (You can list and repent of
any specific sins that you know of in your family
line, if you wish. Examples of sins include anger,
bitterness, lust, adultery, misappropriation of

finances, poverty, early death, disease, addictions, fear, anxiety, lethargy, false idol worship, false religion, depression, mental illness, etc.) *In the name of Jesus, I ask You to please cleanse me in Your blood to remove the effects that these sins and iniquities have had on me and my generational line. I command any connected and related spirits to leave me now in the name of Jesus. I plead the blood of Jesus over me and all of my remaining family line. Amen.*

SOUL TIES

A soul tie is an ungodly connection between two people. For example, if a woman has an ungodly soul tie with her ex-boyfriend, that soul tie may be preventing her from moving into the proper covenant relationship that God has for her, such as her true husband.

Soul ties can be formed many different ways. Fornication or other sexual acts can create a soul tie. Even lustful acts that do not involve sex can still create a soul tie. Homosexual or lesbian relationships can cre- ᴜl tie. Any kind of dominating relationship or ᴛhy relationship—especially one that involves control or manipulation—can create a soul tie. Victims can have soul ties with their abusers. Blood covenants can also create a soul tie.

Any kind of dominating relationship or unhealthy relationship—especially one that involves control or manipulation—can create a soul tie.

Involvement, association, or participation in any false religions, cults, Masonry, clubs, fraternities, sororities, scouts or guides can potentially create a soul tie as well. If the organization or association is one that is filled with sin or based on ungodly principles, it can result in a tie that connects a person with the occult.

Objects can also carry soul ties. For example, an object given to you by someone you were in a wrong relationship with can carry a soul tie between you and that person. This was the case in my own life. I was going to be engaged to a man who was not meant to be my husband. As a promise of our upcoming engagement, he bought me diamonds. Afterward, however, God revealed to me that this relationship was not His will for my life and that I needed to end it.

When we broke up, he did not want the diamonds back. I didn't want to keep them, so I exchanged them for other pieces of jewelry. From these diamonds, I was able to get a set of diamond and pearl earrings, a diamond and pearl ring, and a sapphire and diamond ring. In my mind, I didn't see anything wrong with what I had done. The relationship was broken, as God had wanted, and I had not kept the original jewelry he had given me.

I also had three pieces of new, beautiful, expensive jewelry. Needless to say, I was very happy!

A few years later, while in Bible school, I heard a sermon about ungodly soul ties. Up until this point I was not even aware that such a thing existed. I did not know what a soul tie was, or the effects it could have on a person. The pastor preaching was emphasizing the importance of breaking all ungodly ties in order for us to live completely free. As I was listening to this sermon, God began to deal with me about these three pieces of jewelry. He told me that I had to get rid of them in order to break the soul tie that I had with my ex. God also reminded me of times when I wore the rings and my fingers would burn. I never knew why, but as I was listening to the sermon, God revealed to me it was because this jewelry carried an ungodly soul tie.

This jewelry was very expensive. I struggled to part with it. I even tried to bargain with God. I asked Him if I could sell the jewelry and use the money to go on a mission trip. He said no. God clearly told me to gather all three pieces, and at the next church service put them into the offering plate. I chose to obey and did exactly as He said.

I didn't know it at the time, but God was actually preparing me to meet my true husband by removing this soul tie. The amazing thing was that my then future husband, who was also a student at the same Bible school, saw the ring on my finger before we were ever a couple. God told him that there was a soul tie connected to the ring. He was a bit puzzled as to why God was sharing this information with him. Little did he know we were to be married in the future!

Regardless of what God asks you to do, you need to be obedient. If God is showing you information about an object, even if it has great value like that jewelry, you must do what He tells you. You do not know what you are missing by not listening. A few years after giving up that jewelry, I married my husband, and God supplied a huge diamond ring. I upgraded, and now my jewelry does not have an evil soul tie. What would have happened if I had not obeyed His leading to give up that jewelry? I don't know for sure, but I am so glad I obeyed!

> Regardless of what God asks you to do, you need to be obedient. If God is showing you information about an object, even if it has great value like that jewelry, you must do what He tells you.

It is important that we ask God if there are any ungodly soul ties in our lives. We need to ask Him to break them in the name of Jesus. Are you ready to break any soul ties that have been hindering you? Read this prayer aloud right now:

Breaking Soul Ties Prayer

Dear heavenly Father,

I repent for any ungodly soul ties that I may have created or participated in, whether knowingly or unknowingly. I ask You to please forgive me. In the name of Jesus, I now break and renounce all evil soul ties that I or my generations have had. These include any ungodly soul ties with the Masonic Lodge or any of its orders, ungodly scout or guide organizations, cults or covens, partners I became sexually involved with outside of marriage, partners with which I participated in any ungodly sexual, perverted, or lustful acts, anyone who has ever abused or controlled me in any way, blood buddies, tattoo artists, homosexual or lesbian partners or friends, all close friends and family members (both in my natural family and my spiritual family), spouse, ex-spouse(s), parents, grandparents, great-grandparents, and children. In the name of Jesus, I also break and renounce any evil soul ties with any objects that I may have in my possession. I ask You, God, to show me if I need to get rid of anything that has an ungodly soul tie attached to it. I renounce these and any other evil or ungodly soul ties. I break them and wash them now in the blood of Jesus. Amen.

WITCHCRAFT CURSES

Similar to the way a person can use words to curse, a person can also use witchcraft to curse. Witchcraft can come in many different ways and forms. It can come from a witch or a warlock in the form of a spell, but it can also come from a Christian in the form of charismatic witchcraft—which is essentially when a Christian prays his or her own will over certain situations or people. This often results in prayers of manipulation and control. These types of prayers can result in negative effects for all of the parties involved.

An example of this could be praying something like, "Lord, I want this person as my spouse." That may not be God's will. Instead, you should pray something like, "Lord, please bring me the spouse that You have selected for me." If you begin to pray for a certain person to be your spouse versus praying God's choice for you, the individual you are asking the Lord for may start to feel confused without even understanding why. Your prayers are essentially releasing a curse of confusion over that person and are affecting how he or she feels.

> If you begin to pray for a certain person to be your spouse versus praying God's choice for you, your prayers are essentially releasing a curse of confusion over that person and are affecting how he or she feels.

Witchcraft curses can also affect us if v within our generations, opened the door ᴜ through involvement in any witchcraft or deᴍ activities, such as magic, Ouija boards, voodoo, horoscopes, fortune telling, idol worship, false religions, occult literature, movies, music, or games, martial arts, and so on.

Those under the influence of a witchcraft curse or any connected spirits may experience an interest in or a desire to dabble in witchcraft and the occult themselves—or even feel drawn to New Age, which is a form of witchcraft. They may also struggle with rebellion, or experience difficulty focusing on the things of God. Witchcraft curses can also manifest specifically the way they were created to. For example, a curse of female singlehood may result in every woman within that family line remaining single or unable to stay successfully married.

It is important to address every source of witchcraft, to ensure that any access point that the enemy had is d. The following prayer is one that can assist you g this:

Breaking Witchcraft Curses Prayer

Dear heavenly Father,

I repent for any involvement that I or my generations had in any form of witchcraft. I ask You to please forgive me and my generations of these sins and to wash them with the blood of Jesus. I renounce every covenant, pact, or agreement that I or my generations made with any psychic, occult contact, cult, false religion, false doctrine, satanist, or with satan himself. In the name of Jesus, I break all demonic holds on me in these areas all the way back to Adam and Eve and wash them with the blood of Jesus. In the name of Jesus, I also break any witchcraft curses that have been spoken or sent against me. I cover myself in the blood of Jesus and command all connected and related spirits to leave me. I bless anyone who has ever cursed me. I claim freedom from those curses and their effects now in the name of Jesus. Amen.

UNREPENTED SIN

Earlier in this book, we discussed how both our sins and the sins of our generations can give the enemy access to torment us. This is why it is very important that we repent of our sins and the sins of our generations and make repentance part of our daily lives. Go ahead and use this prayer to repent now:

Repentance Prayer

Dear heavenly Father,
I confess that I have sinned, and I repent. I am sorry for my sins. I ask You to please forgive me

now and to wash me in Your blood. I also confess that my generations have sinned against You, and I repent on behalf of them. I ask You to please forgive them and to wash their sins with the blood of Jesus. I now break any hold that these sins have had on me. I break all resulting and connected curses and spirits and command them to leave me now in the name of Jesus. Amen.

Take a moment and ask the Holy Spirit if there are any specific sins that you need to confess and repent of. In your own words, do so now.

JUDGMENTS

Whether we realize it or not, judgments are very powerful. When we judge someone, it not only negatively affects the person, but it also negatively affects us in the form of a curse. When we release a judgment, it essentially has a boomerang effect—it comes right back to hit us. The New Living Translation of the Bible outlines this in Luke 6:37: *"Do not judge others, and you will not be judged. Do not condemn others, or it will all come back against you...."*

Judgments are not solely verbal. Judgments can also be made internally. We can judge people by how they look, how they dress, or how they talk. We can judge a person's motives incorrectly. If you really examined how frequently you make a judgment, you would probably be shocked! It is such an easy thing to do. It is important that you catch yourself and repent quickly to prevent any negative effects from these judgments. For example, you might look at someone with a weight issue and judge them. Not thinking anything of this, you do not repent or ask for forgiveness.

Before you know it, however, you are struggling with a weight issue yourself.

> Judgments are not solely verbal. Judgments can also be made internally.

Perhaps you judge a couple that is experiencing marital issues. Maybe they are even friends of yours, but you internally judge the success of their marriage and how they treat each other. Your marriage had previously been fine, but now, all of a sudden, you are experiencing those same marital issues as well.

If the times you have judged are coming to your remembrance, go ahead and read this prayer aloud, asking God to wash you clean of any effects those judgments have had on you or on anyone you have judged:

Judgments Prayer

Dear heavenly Father,

I confess that I have judged others, and I realize that judging is a sin. I repent for doing so. I ask You to please forgive me for all the judgments I have made, including those toward family members, friends, spiritual leaders, and political leaders. Please bless all the people I have ever judged. In the name of Jesus, I break those judgments and all curses involved. I command any connected demonic spirits to leave in the name of Jesus. Amen.

A LEVIATHAN SPIRIT

In the next chapter, I will discuss some of the different types of spirits and what their effects can be. I will also briefly touch on one spirit now, as this spirit can block a person's freedom. A Leviathan spirit is mentioned specifically in the Bible in Job 41. Without going into too much detail, Leviathan is essentially a serpent-like spirit. Individuals oppressed by a Leviathan spirit may experience difficulty with Bible study and worshipping God. They may have overall problems concentrating or learning. One of the other things a Leviathan spirit can do is block a person from receiving deliverance. To remove a Leviathan spirit, repent of the sins responsible for inviting the spirit into your life and break any connected curses. You can do this using the following prayer:

Leviathan Prayer

Dear heavenly Father,

I repent of my sins and the sins of my ancestors all the way back to Adam and Eve who allowed the spirit of Leviathan to come and torment me. I am sorry for these sins, and I ask You to please forgive me and wash me in Your blood. In the name of Jesus, I break any curses that may have resulted from these sins and cover them with the blood of Jesus. I command any spirits of Leviathan that may be attacking me as a result of such sins or curses to leave me now in the name of Jesus. Amen.

> If you have read these prayers and you still feel blocked, ask the Lord and see what else He may reveal to you.

These are just some of the blocks that can prevent a person's freedom. Certainly, there are more than what is listed in this book. If you have read these prayers and you still feel blocked, ask the Lord and see what else He may reveal to you. If and when He shows you anything, be sure to repent of it and ask for His liberating power.

CHAPTER 7

WHAT ARE THE TYPES OF SPIRITS?

There are several different types of demonic spirits. Many of them have names that reflect how they make a person feel. A spirit of depression will make a person feel depressed, just as a spirit of anger will make a person feel angry, and so on. Spirits also have ranks, meaning that some have control over others. Spirits can also work together in groups, often called "families" or "nests."

I believe Christians should not become caught up in the intricate details of the demonic realm. While it is certainly necessary for all Christians to have a general knowledge, it is imperative that we do not focus on demonic spirits to the point of fascination or even obsession. Remember that Philippians 4 tells us to keep our eyes focused on what is good and praiseworthy. *When learning about spirits or engaging in deliverance, our primary focus should always be on God.* It should never be on trying to learn every detail about every spirit to the point where we are glorifying satan more than God!

Unfortunately, I have seen people take this to the extreme and enter an unhealthy place of fascination with the demonic realm, thereby losing sight of the power of God and His goodness. When I train others in deliverance ministry, I always stress the importance of worshipping and glorifying God above fixating on any satanic force. Whatever you focus on becomes all that you see. We need to stay focused on God, His love, and His supreme power.

However, I believe a basic knowledge of the demonic realm is important in order to be successful in deliverance ministry. When praying for themselves or for others, Christians should be able to recognize whether or not they are dealing with a spiritual issue. If they are dealing with a spiritual issue, Christians should be able to discern the nature of that issue, so they can pray accordingly.

> Whatever you focus on becomes all that you see. We need to stay focused on God, His love, and His supreme power. However, I believe a basic knowledge of the demonic realm is important in order to be successful in deliverance ministry.

One of the gifts God makes available to us—and one of the gifts I use when ministering—is the discerning of spirits, as mentioned in First Corinthians 12:10. Essentially, by using this gift with the power of the Holy Spirit, we can know if we have encountered a spiritual issue. Often this gift can manifest through feelings and emotions. For example, while you are ministering to a person, God may allow you to feel a pain in your body where there was no pain prior. He may do this to tell you where the spirit affecting the person is located, so you can command it to leave from that location.

God can also show you things through dreams and visions, giving you indicators about a demonic spirit that you may be encountering. He can also speak right to your spirit in His still, small voice or by using the Bible. God can communicate with you in many ways, thereby activating the gift of discerning of spirits within you. You can then act on what you are discerning, so you can obtain freedom from any associated oppression.

If we try to use our logical minds to determine what the spiritual issue is, that leaves significant room for error. If we use the gift of discerning of spirits, however, we will be much more accurate in determining the problem. When ministering to clients, I give them an opportunity to tell me about issues they are struggling with. While they are talking, I listen to the Holy Spirit and use this gift to discern what types of demonic spirits are at the root of their issues. Maybe the pain a person is experiencing in his or her joints is not being caused by a spirit of infirmity but rather a spirit of bitterness, which requires that person to forgive before freedom can come.

Numerous spirits can cause the same symptoms, making the gift of discernment very important.

Sometimes I will even have a dream the night prior to ministering to a person. In that dream, God will reveal to me exactly what is causing his or her oppression, thereby making the session the next day very effective right from the start. As Christians, we should be asking God to increase our measure of revelation and discernment, so we can successfully maintain our own freedom and help others receive theirs.

> As Christians, we should be asking God to increase our measure of revelation and discernment, so we can successfully maintain our own freedom and help others receive theirs.

SPIRITS ENCOUNTERED MOST OFTEN

In brief detail, I will now explain some of the spirits I encounter most often when ministering to Christians.

- **Rejection**. This is probably the most common spirit I come across. If you are alive and breathing, you have likely been rejected by someone. Not only can this spirit make a person feel rejected, but it can also cause feelings of abandonment, being unwanted, hurt, emotional pain, or abortion. A spirit of rejection can also cause a person to live with a fear of being rejected to the point where it affects his or her ability to maintain healthy relationships.

- **Bitterness.** If a person is oppressed by a spirit of bitterness, that person may experience feelings of anger, rage, resentment, hatred, rebellion, or destruction. Bitterness may also cause an inability to submit to authority or to forgive. It can also manifest as a physical problem, such as joint pain or arthritis.

- **Depression.** A spirit of depression will do just that—cause a person to feel depressed. It can also bring forth feelings of despair, discouragement, hopelessness, suicide, insomnia, grief, or false guilt.

- **Rejection in the Womb.** A spirit of rejection in the womb can transfer to a person while he or she is in the womb, especially if the person's mother or another family member did not want the child or wanted the child to be of the opposite sex. Similar to a spirit of rejection, individuals oppressed by a spirit of rejection in the womb may experience feelings of deep hurt, sorrow, perpetual pain, or grief. They may also experience lust, sensuality, and other unclean sexual tendencies.

- **Deception.** A spirit of deception will deceive people about God. Deception spirits often oppress those who have practiced a false religion or cult, have read false literature, or have come from generations who participated in any of these things. Those oppressed by a spirit of deception may experience feelings of rejection, confusion, fear, self-hate, doubt, and manipulation. A spirit of deception will also make individuals oblivious to the fact that they are being deceived.

- **Anxiety.** A spirit of anxiety will cause a person to feel anxious. It can cause panic attacks, uneasiness, restlessness, intense fears, palpitations, an inability to relax, headaches, dizziness, paranoia, muscle spasms, nausea, diarrhea, or other physical disturbances.

- **Fear.** A spirit of fear can cause a person to feel fearful, anxious, worried, paralyzed, or traumatized. It can also cause a person to develop many phobias, or to make all of his or her decisions from a place of fear.

- **Pride.** A spirit of pride can cause arrogance, judging, criticism, and faultfinding. Those who are oppressed by a spirit of pride may have an ego issue or walk out a life of selfishness.

- **Insecurity.** Insecurity often works alongside pride. Those suffering with a spirit of insecurity may feel lonely, timid, shy, rejected, or inferior. They may also walk in a place of jealousy or self-pity.

- **Asmodeus.** This is a spirit with an assignment to break up marriages or other covenant relationships. Those struggling with this spirit may experience greed, pride, rejection, lust, restlessness, a barren womb, jealousy, rage, extreme excesses, or overpowering tendencies. They may also experience much strife and discord in their covenant relationships.

- **Death.** A spirit of death will try to cause a person to die. It may manifest itself as trying to bring death to that person's physical body, emotional state, spiritual life, dreams, goals, family, or finances. Those oppressed by a spirit of death may experience thoughts of suicide, murder, or recklessness. Afflicted individuals may develop a death wish, or an unnatural and ungodly fascination with death in general.

- **Gluttony.** A spirit of gluttony will disrupt a person's eating habits and can manifest in many different ways. It can cause a person to eat too much, too little, or in an unhealthy manner. It can cause addictions to one particular food or food group. It can cause a person to eat unnaturally in an attempt to be healed emotionally or cope with pain. A spirit of gluttony can cause problems such as obesity, anorexia, bulimia, self-hate, anger, anxiety, death, fear, bitterness, self-rejection, or starvation.

- **Retaliation.** A spirit of retaliation may attack individuals after they have done something for God—or right before they are about to. Generally speaking, spirits of retaliation can cause destruction, hurt, spite, hatred, distraction, and cruelty.

- **Mental Illness.** A spirit of mental illness can cause a person to feel like he or she is going crazy. It can bring forth things like insanity, bipolar disorder, retardation, madness, paranoia, schizophrenia, and hallucinations.

- **Familiar Spirits.** Familiar spirits are spirits that have been in a person's generational line or land of origin. They can be any spirit that the person's mother, father, or generations struggled with. Common familiar spirits include witchcraft, addictions, lust, perversions, insecurity, anger, pride, and rebellion.

- **Antichrist.** Antichrist spirits will cause a person to hate or oppose the things of God or the Spirit. Antichrist spirits can bring forth rage, anger, and bitterness. They can also cause a person to be very argumentative.

- **Unforgiveness.** We discussed the spirit of unforgiveness earlier, but as a quick recap, this spirit will try to block a person from forgiving. Unforgiveness can lead to hate, resentment, and bitterness.

- **Addictions.** A spirit of addiction can manifest in many forms. Essentially it causes individuals to become addicted to something, thereby giving this spirit control over them by using their addiction against them. Some of the most common manifestations of this spirit are addictions to drugs, alcohol, lying, gambling, pain killers, and sexual acts. Addiction spirits can also cause feelings of anguish and captivity.

- **Infirmity.** As discussed previously, a spirit of infirmity will cause a person to be sick or have a physical problem in his or her body. Infirmity spirits can cause arthritis, lupus, heart problems, viruses, infections, skin diseases, migraines, nerve issues, cancer, ulcers, or an unexplained and unjustified pain, among other things. While not all illnesses are spiritual, many do have spiritual roots or spiritual components at least to some degree.

- **Inheritance.** A spirit of inheritance is anything that a person inherited from his or her generations. Examples of inherited spirits are control, rejection, witchcraft, violence, rage, cancer, death, fear, alcoholism, and jealousy, just to name a few.

- **Transferred Spirits.** These are spirits that can be transferred from one person to another, whether generationally, environmentally, through a soul tie, or through a blood covenant. They can also be spirits that have been transferred sexually, or through touch, molestation, or rape. Transferred spirits can include lust, promiscuity, rape, and control.

- **Sexual Impurity.** A spirit of sexual impurity can cause a variety of sexual tendencies, sinful behaviors, and issues, including lust, homosexuality or lesbianism, sexual fantasies, masturbation, oral sex, bestiality, orgies, rape, exposure, fornication, abortion, pornography addictions, child molestation, frigidity, or promiscuity.

- **Leviathan.** As discussed previously, a spirit of Leviathan is mentioned in the Bible in Job 41. This spirit can cause issues with Bible study, worship, or the things of God and the Spirit. It can cause problems learning, feelings of depression, brooding, haughtiness, frustration, and impatience. It can also make a person stubborn and unteachable, or become a block for a person to receive freedom.

- **Python.** A Python spirit will try to squeeze the life out of a person, church, or ministry. It can bring forth feelings of fatigue, confusion, weariness, frustration, heaviness, oppression, greed, division, grief, control, and deceit.

- **Witchcraft / Occult.** These demonic spirits can manifest in many different forms, such as antichrist behaviors, hypnotism, voodoo, occult fears, false dreams, automatic handwriting, hearing voices, spirit guides, trances, numerology, auras, and Kabala.

- **Jezebel / Control.** Unlike Jezebel in the Bible, this spirit does not have a gender and can manifest through a man or a woman. The goal of a Jezebel spirit is to control others in order to gain more power and influence for itself. It will try to stop the work of God's true prophets or try to eliminate them entirely. A Jezebel spirit will come against prophetic people and churches, robbing them of visions and dreams from God. A Jezebel spirit hates authority and will only be submissive to gain control. It wants to be in control of everything from finances to how the Holy Spirit moves. A Jezebel spirit can bring a person or a church to a place of confusion, division, discord, disunity, striving, or disobedience. A person influenced by a Jezebel spirit may experience degrees of deception, pride, rebellion, and perversion. He or she may be unteachable, uncorrectable, critical toward leadership, rebellious, or controlling. That person may also try to use intimidation, manipulation, or flattery to get his or her way and may try to turn people within the church against each other.

These are just some of the more common demonic spirits that I encounter when ministering to Christians. Again, it is important that you do not spend too much time focusing on the spirits themselves—or on trying to figure out what spirit your spouse has! Instead, focus on Jesus, walk in the authority that He has given you, and thank Him for your freedom!

CHAPTER 8

DO CHILDREN NEED DELIVERANCE?

As Christian adults, we can receive freedom by understanding who we are in Christ, repenting of our sins, forgiving those who have hurt us, and exercising the authority that He has given us. We can do this because we are adults and understand how to...but what about a child? A baby? We understand now that spirits can pass generationally. That means even a newborn can experience demonic oppression. How does a child receive freedom?

We know that Jesus loves the little children. He would not leave them without a way to be liberated. In Luke 18:16 (NIV), Jesus says, *"Let the little children come to me, and do not hinder them, for the kingdom of God belongs to such as these."* I think it is safe to assume that it is absolutely His desire for children to be set free.

Recently, I have experienced an increase in the number of parents requesting freedom ministry for their children. Demonic spirits can most definitely pass into children—even at the moment of conception or while developing in the womb. Any generational spirits, any word curses spoken over the child, or anything the child's mother is struggling with can potentially transfer to the baby while in the womb. Any trauma during the child's birth or any neglect the child may have experienced from doctors or nurses in the delivery room can cause spiritual oppression. Spirits can also transfer to babies and children in the same manners by which they can transfer to adults—environmentally, through inappropriate touch, etc.

Many schools are experiencing increases in bullying. When a child bullies another child, often that behavior is the result of a spirit of anger, intimidation, or domination that is working through the child. In addition to bullying, we have also seen an increase in other acts of anger and violence among children—sometimes to the point where parents are exasperated and do not know how to handle their kids. We are also seeing more and more reports of sexual addictions beginning at a young age. These addictions can be the result of a child being exposed to a spirit of sexual impurity.

I remember vividly a time when my husband called me from the grocery store with a question about something that we needed. While he was on the phone with me, minding his own business, a young child came running and screaming toward him. This child threw himself at my husband's feet and began foaming at the mouth. The child fell into a zombie-like state. My husband was shocked, as was the mother of the child. She came running after her son and apologized profusely for his behavior.

> Many schools are experiencing increases in bullying. When a child bullies another child, often that behavior is the result of a spirit of anger, intimidation, or domination that is working through the child.

The mother attempted to pick up her son from the floor. He wasn't cooperating, so she dragged him away, in total shock and dismay. While she was doing so, she repeatedly apologized to my husband and informed him that her child had never acted this way before. My husband knew exactly what had just happened. The demonic spirits in that child recognized the Spirit of God in both my husband and me, and manifested! Remember the time Jesus stepped out of the boat and the demoniac ran and threw himself at His feet? You can read this story in Mark 5:2-13. Clearly this is still happening today.

Children nowadays are being exposed to movies, music, and video games filled with violence, witchcraft, and explicit sexual content. All this ungodliness can become entry points for a child to experience demonic oppression. Even some of what is being taught in schools today does not line up with the Word of God, and if not handled properly can also become an open door for a child to be attacked.

> Children nowadays are being exposed to movies, music, and video games filled with violence, witchcraft, and explicit sexual content. All this ungodliness can become entry points for a child to experience demonic oppression.

BEWARE THE DECEIVER

Nowadays, there is so much evil being widely accepted as good. Satan is a deceiver. If he can use something masquerading as innocent to carry out his plans, then he will do just that. Unfortunately, he likes to prey upon innocent children.

In my household, my husband and I are extremely careful as to what our son is exposed to. We try our best to monitor what he watches, reads, and plays. Sometimes I wish I could keep him in a bubble! That is, of course, unrealistic. We teach him what is right and what is wrong, according to the standards laid out in God's Word. As parents, we must trust that he will make decisions based on the truth that we are teaching him.

When he was quite young, the biggest craze at his school was Pokémon trading cards. I remember the first time he came home with some cards that his friend had given him. Looking at them, I was appalled! These cards had images of creatures that looked so demonic. I explained to my son that we did not want these cards in our home because they were not good and would most likely give him nightmares. I just knew that these cards had demonic spirits attached to them, and I did not want those spirits affecting my son or our household.

I'm pretty sure these trading cards also had a demonic pull on them, enticing children to the place of obsession. We struggled for a few months with getting my son to stop coming home with these cards. I would always allow him to choose whether or not to throw them away. Eventually, he did stop bringing them home.

Later on, I actually heard that some schools had banned the cards all together because students were fighting over them and became unable to focus on their studies. This was a confirmation to me that these cards were indeed an example of an object that carried a demonic spirit. Objects are just one entry point that satan can use to demonically oppress children to the point where they may require deliverance. The devil uses the same tactics on both adults and children.

If there is one thing I have noticed from ministering deliverance to children versus adults, it is that God is always so gracious when it comes to a child's freedom. Typically, it is simple and quick. Often the baby or child will not even know it is happening. Parents, or those who have authority over the child, can pray and claim deliverance on the child's behalf. To avoid scaring the child, this can even be done while the child is sleeping.

> God is always so gracious when it comes to a child's freedom. Typically, it is simple and quick. Often the baby or child will not even know it is happening.

Parents can begin by asking the Holy Spirit what to pray and if there are any specific spiritual issues that should be prayed off the child. Sometimes it may be obvious, like if your child is always angry, pray off a spirit of anger. Sometimes it may not be as clear. Again, it is important to remember not to spend too much time focusing on the spirits themselves, or on trying to analyze what might be there. You do not have to know exactly what is oppressing the child in order for it to leave!

The following is a prayer that parents can pray over their child:

Parent's Prayer Over Child

Dear heavenly Father,

Thank You for _____ (name of child) and for giving me the honor of being his/her parent. I come to You on behalf of my child and ask You to deliver this precious child of Yours. I repent for any generational sins that may be affecting my child (name specific sins if you wish) *and I command any connected or related curses to be broken in the name of Jesus. I command any connected or related spirits to leave my child now in the name of Jesus. I command any other spirits affecting my child, regardless of the source, to leave him/ her now in the name of Jesus* (name specific spirits if you wish). *I plead the blood of Jesus over my child, and command everything that is not of God to lift and leave him/her now in the name of Jesus. God, I ask You to please fill my child with spirits of peace and joy, and to bring my child any healing that he/she may need. Thank You, Lord, for setting my child, Your child, free. Amen.*

This prayer, or similar ones, can be prayed over children of any age. As children get older, however, it is important to teach them how to pray for themselves and how to call on God for their own freedom.

Next you will find two prayers that can be given to children to read aloud over themselves, categorized by the child's age:

Child's Prayer (10 & younger)

Dear Jesus,

I love You, and I am sorry for all the bad things I have done. Please forgive me. I belong to You, and I want to live for You. I forgive everyone who has hurt me, made me mad, or made me cry. I cover myself with the blood of Jesus. I put on the armor of God. The Holy Spirit leads and guides me and helps me know right from wrong. Satan has no control over me.

God, I ask You, in the name of Jesus, to remove the things that hurt me or cause me to do wrong. God, I also ask You to remove these things from my bedroom and my house, and to send angels to surround me and protect me from the things that want to bother me. God, please help me in every area of my life and take care of me and my family everywhere we go. In Jesus' name, amen.

Child's Prayer (11 & older)

Dear Jesus,

I love You, and I repent for all the bad things I have done. Please forgive me and cleanse me in Your blood. I belong to You and I want to live for

You. I choose to break all ties with satan and to close any access points that I may have opened to him. I forgive everyone who has hurt me or wronged me. I bless them, and I ask You to take all of the hurt and pain away. I cover myself with the blood of Jesus. I put on the armor of God. I ask for angels to protect and surround me everywhere I go. The Holy Spirit leads me, guides me, and helps me know right from wrong. Satan is not in control of me—in Jesus I have all authority over him and his demons.

God, I ask You, in the name of Jesus, to remove the things that hurt me or cause me to do wrong. I command anything that is not of God to leave me now in the name of Jesus. I also ask You, God, to remove any bad spirits from my bedroom and my house. If there is any object that I own that I need to get rid of, I ask You to show me and to help me get rid of it. God, I ask You to protect me from the things that want to bother me. God, please help me and bless me in every area of my life. Help me to learn, grow, and prosper in the things of You. Please take care of me and my family everywhere we go and help us serve You all the days of our lives. In Jesus' name, amen.

By having your child read a prayer daily, it will ensure that your child is communicating regularly with God. These prayers can also teach children how to call on Him for their freedom. As parents, guardians, or caregivers, ask God to speak to you and guide you as to how you can help your child walk in freedom. Be on watch for any transferred spirits, and command those transferred spirits to leave your child in the name of Jesus.

> God knows how much you love your child. First and foremost, your child is actually His child.

God knows how much you love your child. First and foremost, your child is actually His child. How much more, then, does He want to partner with you to keep your child free? Infinitely and eternally more.

CHAPTER 9

CAN SPIRITS AFFECT ME AFTER BEING CAST OUT?

Receiving deliverance ministry is not a quick fix. It does not automatically make a person immune to being affected by demonic spirits. Even following deliverance, a Christian can still experience demonic influences. The difference now, however, is that these demons are affecting from an external position rather than an internal position. Let's discuss some different ways that a Christian can still encounter demonic affliction post-deliverance and the remedies for each potential encounter.

SPIRITS OF RETALIATION POST-DELIVERANCE

Often when a person receives freedom, he or she will feel great initially but then shortly afterward may feel symptoms returning. For example, if God sets a person free from depression, that person might feel completely happy for a few days; but then all of a sudden, that person may wake up one morning feeling very depressed. This is when the enemy will lie and try to convince the individual that he or she was never free in the first place. Often, what is actually happening is the demonic spirit is just around the person, in the atmosphere, trying to get back inside. Even externally, demonic spirits can cause individuals to experience the same feelings that they would experience if that spirit was inside them. This is not uncommon.

The young lady I mentioned earlier who was set free from a spirit of infirmity experienced symptoms returning the very next day. This spirit was no longer inside her, but it was around her and was causing her to feel the same type of oppression. In her case, the difference now was that she could exercise her authority in Christ and command it to leave in the name of Jesus. When she did that, the spirit left, and all of those symptoms disappeared.

> When we feel we are under attack, we need to use our weapons of spiritual warfare and live a holy and consecrated life to maintain our freedom.

Recognizing the tactics of the enemy can be helpful in maintaining freedom, but it is not enough. When we feel we are under attack, we need to use our weapons of spiritual warfare and live a holy and consecrated life to maintain our freedom. We will discuss this in more detail in the next chapter.

SPIRITS IN AN ATMOSPHERE

Atmospheres are one way that demonic spirits can still affect Christians post-deliverance. As much as a Christian can have a demon, atmospheres and physical spaces can also have demons. For example, a casino building will most likely be filled with spirits of addiction and mammon. A bar may be filled with spirits of lust, sexual impurity, and alcoholism. Essentially the activities and sins permitted within any particular location open a door for the enemy to dwell within that location, just as our own unrepented sins open a door for the enemy to dwell within us.

Atmospheres of all kinds can have demonic activity present, including our own homes. What we watch, what we listen to, how we speak, what we do—all of these can be gateways that leave our home unprotected and exposed.

Even after receiving deliverance, Christians can still be very affected by atmospheres that have a demonic presence. For example, maybe you are feeling great when you go to visit your friend. Then all of a sudden, as soon as you walk through the door you feel angry and irritated. You might think that you are dealing with a demonic spirit of anger yourself. Most likely what is happening, however, is you are picking up on something that is in your friend's home and you are being affected by that spirit. It could also be something that your friend might personally be struggling with.

How Christians typically handle demonic spirits present in an atmosphere varies, depending on exactly where they are and what authority they have over that location. A person is likely going to handle spirits in a public place differently than spirits in his or her own home.

In a public place, you want to focus more on keeping yourself free from spirits versus keeping the whole location free from spirits. We cannot be responsible for everything in the world around us, but we can take responsibility over how we interact with it. By using the personal warfare and cleansing strategies outlined in the next chapter, we can keep ourselves free from any demonic spirits that want to attack or transfer to us from any place we have visited.

> We cannot be responsible for everything in the world around us, but we can take responsibility over how we interact with it.

In a private location like your home, however, it is very important to regularly "clean" in the spirit. Not

only can demonic activity in your home cause y
tional disturbances, but it can also affect your ᴜ......,
receive revelation, dreams, or visions from God. It can
hinder your prayer life, your ability to worship, or your
comprehension of the Bible.

The following prayer is one you can say within
your home regularly to drive out any demonic spirits. Reading this prayer, or similar ones, in each room
of your home is a great way to ensure that your space
stays clear:

House Cleansing Prayer

Dear heavenly Father,

*Thank You for cleansing me and my home in the
blood of Jesus. I ask You to send Your angels into
this place to sweep through and remove anything
residing here that is not of You. In Jesus' name, I
command any demonic spirits that are taking up
residence in the foundation, walls, furnishings, or
anywhere else in my home to leave now.*

*I command any demonic spirits that were trans-
ferred, have been sent on assignment, came in
with any person, or entered through sin, including through any song, TV show, or movie, to leave
this place now in the name of Jesus.* (You can also
list any specific spirits that you feel are in your
home if you wish, commanding them out in the
name of Jesus.) *I take authority over the space*

You have given me. I thank You, God, for sending Your angels to cleanse it with the precious blood of Jesus. I also ask, God, that You post angels throughout this home and around the property, to protect against any future demonic intrusions. Amen.

In addition to this prayer, you should also regularly implement other spiritual warfare tactics, such as anointing each room with oil, pleading the blood of Jesus around your property, and playing anointed worship music throughout your home. These are great tools to keep your house peaceful and full of God's glory.

SPIRITS FROM OTHER PEOPLE

Christians can also be affected by demons if someone they are talking to, engaging with, or praying for is currently under demonic attack. For example, if you are on the phone with someone struggling with anxiety, after hanging up you might feel anxious yourself. Again, in this case, most likely what is happening is the demonic spirit is not in you, it has just transferred from the person you were in conversation with. This is why proper cleansing and regular self-deliverance is so important.

In everyday life, when we are discerning or being affected by a spirit from another person, often God is not showing us this because He wants us to immediately cast the spirit out of that person. It is so important that when you discern something, you ask God for wisdom about what you are to do with this information. Every situation is different. What God wants you to do may not necessarily be what you want to do, but it is important that you follow His leading to ensure the best possible outcome not only for yourself but also for the other person involved.

> Proper cleansing and regular self-deliverance is so important.

Often, when we discern something, what God wants us to do is take that information to Him in prayer. Sometimes He tells us something about another person not because we are meant to tell others about it, but because He wants us to be interceding for that person. I have noticed that the more we are responsible with what we discern, the more God will reveal information to us because we have proven to Him that we can be trusted with what He shares.

When a demonic spirit attacking a person affects you personally, it is important to do spiritual warfare to cleanse yourself. For example, if after talking to someone struggling with sexual issues you are bombarded with sexual thoughts, you need to pray those spirits off of yourself immediately.

SPIRITS FROM OBJECTS

Another way spirits can affect Christians post-deliverance is through objects they possess. Objects themselves can carry spirits also—especially objects of the occult or witchcraft. More obvious examples would be objects like Ouija boards, tarot cards, crystal balls, and other objects used in the practice of witchcraft. Less obvious examples include New Age literature and books, DVDs of movies that are filled with violence, sexual impurity, or witchcraft, and video games with violence, blood, or gore. Demonic spirits can also be attached to any object that has been specifically cursed. This could be something like a sculpture or a carving that was cursed by the person who created it.

If you use logic, it can be difficult to know if any object within your possession is carrying a demonic spirit. You need to ask the Holy Spirit to show you. When you discern that an object is carrying a demonic spirit, the solution will vary based on whether or not the object is yours. If the object is not yours, I do not advise you to throw it away, out of respect for the person it belongs to. You can, however, exercise your authority in Christ and command all demonic spirits to leave the object.

If the object belongs to you, the solution is very simple—get rid of it! Do not give it to somebody else, do not sell it, do not hide it away in your basement, and do not donate it to a thrift store. If it is not good for you, that means it is not good for anyone! Destroy it. Throw it out, burn it, or break it. Ask the Holy Spirit how He would have you get rid of it. Whatever the Spirit says to do— do it!

If the Holy Spirit is telling you to get rid of something, it is not to hurt you. It is to help you. God cares about you, and no object is worth putting above Him or above your freedom. When objects with evil spirits are allowed to reside in your possession, they become a snare and they allow the devil access to torment you. God may even show you that an object you consider very special, such as a family heirloom or a piece of jewelry, has a demonic spirit attached to it. He will not force you to get rid of it; but if He is showing you, it is because He loves you and He wants you to be free.

> If the Holy Spirit is telling you to get rid of something, it is not to hurt you. It is to help you.

Ultimately, it is your choice. Often when you do take that step to get rid of it—especially if the enemy has really been fighting you on it—you will experience great freedom instantly. This was the case in my own life.

In the beginning of my marriage, my husband and I experienced a lot of strife, anger, and tension. It seemed like we were constantly fighting. One particular time, while we were in the midst of a heated argument, I looked over into the dining room at a picture on the wall, one I had inherited from my father. This picture was a pencil drawing of a beautiful group of horses running together. I had looked at this picture many times; but now for the first time, I saw that it was actually a drawing within a drawing. The drawing within the drawing was hidden; my husband and I had never seen it before. But now, it looked so clear—right in the middle of the horses were five evil, angry faces staring back at us.

I couldn't believe it! These faces reflected everything going on in my home between me and my husband. Depictions of anger, rage, fighting, and strife were evident in this picture. Now I knew why we had been fighting so much. This picture had been releasing evil spirits right into our home, and we had been oblivious to it! I asked my husband to remove it and take it to a place where he could burn it. He immediately took it off the wall and did just that. I did not go with him, but he shared with me that when he threw it into the fire, five evil voices screamed as it burned. Crazy, right?! Once that picture was removed from our home, the strife and arguing left too.

When encountering objects that potentially have spirits attached, a great rule of thumb—when in doubt, throw it out! If there is an object you are unsure of, it is always better to be safe than sorry. Remember that as a Christian who is filled with the Holy Spirit, you

have God inside you. He may be trying to spea
through a feeling. That feeling may be Him telling y
to get rid of it. Remember, no object is worth sacrificing
the freedom that Christ died for you to have. When in
doubt, throw it out!

Use the following prayer to ask the Holy Spirit if
there are any objects within your possession that are
carrying evil spirits or providing an entry point for
the enemy.

Objects With Demonic Spirits Prayer

Dear heavenly Father,
Thank You, Lord, for caring about my freedom.
I ask for Your Holy Spirit to fill this place. Please
show me if there are any objects within my home
or among my possessions that have demonic spir-
its attached to them. Please also reveal what You
would have me do with these objects and super-
naturally empower me to obey Your direction
without hesitation. I ask this now in the name of
Jesus. Amen.

Pause and allow the Holy Spirit to show you
any objects with spirits attached, along with the
action He would have you take. Once He shows
you, act immediately before the enemy attacks with
contradicting thoughts.

SPIRITUAL ATTACKS

Receiving deliverance does not make satan disappear. Even if you keep all reentry points closed following deliverance, the devil may still try to attack. As a Christian, you can expect this to happen at some point—especially if you are trying to advance the Kingdom of God!

> Receiving deliverance does not make satan disappear. Even if you keep all reentry points closed following deliverance, the devil may still try to attack.

Spiritual attacks are one way the enemy tries to stop Christians in their tracks. For example, if you are scheduled to be on the prayer team at your church on Sunday morning, you may feel downright awful on Saturday night. This does not necessarily mean there is something wrong with you. Most likely what is happening is satan is using his demonic spirits to attack you. His purpose is to discourage you and stop you from going to church altogether, successfully ensuring that you will not be used to minister to God's people. It is imperative to understand satan's tactics so that we can be better equipped to recognize and overcome them.

SPIRITS THROUGH UNREPENTED SIN

If we provide the enemy with a legal right to attack us following deliverance, you better believe that is exactly what he will do. Deliverance is a process. Once we have received freedom, we then need to walk out a lifestyle reflective of that freedom. For example, if you have been delivered from a smoking addiction but then choose to smoke a cigarette, the spirit of addiction that God freed you from now has an open invitation to come right back in.

We all sin, and you may slip up following freedom ministry. The important thing is that you repent quickly and get those sins under the blood, as unrepented sin gives the enemy an invitation to return. The other important part is that you make the choice in your heart to change your ways. If you are fully, completely, and honestly committed to living free from the sinful behaviors you have been delivered from—and are asking God to help you do so—He will always provide you with a route of escape whenever you are being ʳed. The more you take His direction, the easier it ome. This is how lifestyles are changed.

If demonic spirits are attacking you because you have open doors in your life—shut them! Being Christians and having access to the grace and forgiveness of God does not provide us with a free ticket to sin whenever we feel like it. Being a Christian involves self-discipline and making choices that line up with the Word and the will of God. There is a difference between making a mistake and constantly choosing to sin.

> *What shall we say, then? Shall we go on sinning so that grace may increase? By no means! We are those who have died to sin; how can we live in it any longer?* (Romans 6:1-2 NIV)

If demonic spirits are attacking you because you have open doors in your life—shut them!

If you want to maintain freedom from demonic affliction post-deliverance, you need to choose to stay free from sin. If that means ending certain relationships—end them. Maybe you need an accountability partner. Maybe you need to put an alert system on your electronic devices, one that will notify someone if you go onto an X-rated site. Make your lifestyle choices line up with your decision to keep all doors closed. You can do it!

Though there are many ways a Christian can be affected by demonic spirits following deliverance, it is important not to live in fear or become obsessed with the possibility of spirits around you. Spirits are nothing to be afraid of because we, as Christians, have been given the tools to combat them. We can be even more effective with these tools post-deliverance, because our own "junk" is no longer there to hinder us.

CHAPTER 10

HOW DO I MAINTAIN MY FREEDOM?

As mentioned earlier, receiving deliverance ministry is not a quick fix. After God sets us free, we have a responsibility to walk out that freedom. God has given us the tools and strategies necessary to do this, but it is our responsibility to apply them to our lives.

Maintaining our freedom involves both understanding and engaging in spiritual warfare. Remember, our enemy is not a person. Our enemy is satan, and we must fight him in the spirit with spiritual tools. The Bible outlines this in Ephesians 6:12 (NIV):

> *For our struggle is not against flesh and blood, but against the rulers, against the authorities, against the powers of this dark world and against the spiritual forces of evil in the heavenly realms.*

If we are fighting in the spirit, our weapons must also be in the spirit in order for them to be effective.

> Maintaining our freedom involves both understanding and engaging in spiritual warfare. Remember, our enemy is not a person. Our enemy is satan.

YOUR SPIRITUAL WEAPONS

The following are some of the spiritual weapons that God has provided for you to use against the enemy:

- Fully consecrate your life to Christ.
- Confess your sins and repent.
- Forgiveness.
- Attend church and maintain proper spiritual alignment.
- Bind and loose, declare and decree.
- Pray—especially in your heavenly language (tongues).
- Read the Bible.
- Take Communion.
- Apply anointing oil.
- Praise and worship.
- Put on the armor of God.
- Ask for angels.
- Use the name and the blood of Jesus.
- Pray the daily warfare prayer.

Now let's examine how you can properly apply each of these spiritual weapons to your life in order to maintain your freedom.

Fully Consecrate Your Life to Christ

A fully consecrated life—one that is completely surrendered to God in every area—becomes an offensive weapon against the enemy. If satan is not provided with an entry point into your life, this immediately lessens his power over you. This will, in turn, make all your other weapons more effective because God's hands are not tied by your own sin, meaning He has room to move on your behalf.

> A fully consecrated life—one that is completely surrendered to God in every area—becomes an offensive weapon against the enemy.

The word "consecrated" can be defined as making something sacred or dedicating something to a particular purpose. As Christians, we need to make sure our lives are as pure and clean as possible, while also being fully dedicated to God. We must walk separate from the world. We cannot have one foot in the church and one foot in the world, while still expecting to win the battle.

The Bible talks about this in Leviticus 20:7 (NIV), where it says, *"Consecrate yourselves and be holy, because I am the Lord your God."* We also read about it in

Second Corinthians 6:17 (NKJV), which says, *"Therefore 'Come out from among them, and be separate,' says the Lord. 'Do not touch what is unclean, and I will receive you.'"* Living a clean life is living a good life.

Confess Your Sins and Repent

We are not perfect, and sin happens. If we want to walk in freedom, however, it is important that we confess our sins and repent in a timely manner. If we get our sins under the blood of Jesus quickly, this prevents torment.

The Bible tells us we can even sin in our minds without any accompanying outward action (Matthew 5:28). Therefore, we need to ask God daily to show us any sins that we have committed so that we can confess them and repent. It may seem like a simple act, but it is a mighty weapon against the enemy.

Forgiveness

As we discussed earlier, unforgiveness will block freedom. This is not limited to just choosing not to forgive. It is also applicable when we do not actively forgive others regularly. We need to make sure we are asking God to search our hearts daily so that He can highlight those we need to forgive. When He shows us, we need to choose to forgive immediately. By doing so, we enable God to move on our behalf.

Attend Church and Maintain Proper Spiritual Alignment

Another great way to maintain your freedom is to be plugged into a Spirit-filled church and attend regularly. Not only will the right church provide you with teaching and training, it will also provide you with proper spiritual covering. Everyone should have a pastor to whom they are accountable—even pastors should have pastors. The Word of God says that your leaders keep watch over your soul (Hebrews 13:17).

The Christian walk was never meant to be done alone. God instructs us not to forsake the assembling of ourselves (Hebrews 10:25). When we isolate ourselves, we become like lone sheep—much easier for a wolf to attack and devour. For our own protection, we need other Christians and strong spiritual leaders in our lives.

As we walk out our freedom, we may experience demonic attacks that are overwhelming. This is when we need to ask for prayer. If we are already properly plugged into a church, we can easily access someone can pray for us. Attending church regularly is great way to hear the Word of God preached and taught so that we are in a better position to win the war.

Proper spiritual alignment is not just something you need within your church life. It must be present in every facet of your life. This includes your family life, which must align with what is outlined in the Bible. According to God's Word, the husband is at the head of the household, followed by the wife who is submitted to him, followed by the children. The Bible outlines this in First Peter 3:1-2 (NIV):

> *Wives, in the same way submit yourselves to your own husbands so that, if any of them do not believe the word, they may be won over without words by the behavior of their wives, when they see the purity and reverence of your lives.*

Proper spiritual alignment is not just something you need within your church life. It must be present in every facet of your life.

This alignment is for proper spiritual protection. If it is out of order, the family unit becomes vulnerable to attacks. Submission is not a bad word. Essentially, submission is a way of coming under the protection of another person—which, when you are in a spiritual war, is not a bad thing to do!

Bind and Loose, Declare and Decree

Your tongue is a powerful weapon against the enemy. The Bible tells us that our tongues carry the power of both life and death and that we will eat the fruit of what we speak (Proverbs 18:21).

When we are under demonic attack, we need to speak aloud against it. Whatever we are discerning, we need to bind it and command it to leave us in the name of Jesus. For example, if you are feeling confused or discerning a spirit of confusion, you could say aloud: "Spirit of confusion, I bind you and command you to leave me in the name of Jesus." You must use the name of Jesus. After you have said this aloud, you need to loose what you do want, which is typically the exact opposite of what was just bound. For example, after removing confusion you could say something like, "In the name of Jesus, I loose peace and clarity."

Once you have bound and loosed, you should now declare and decree. This can involve prophesying over yourself, reading Scriptures aloud, and speaking God's truth about the situation into the atmosphere. For example, after binding confusion and loosing peace, you could say, "I declare and decree that I am smart and that I think clearly. I have the mind of Christ, and I dwell on the good and not the negative."

Speaking negatively or coming into agreement with negative thoughts can bring forth "death"; but if we verbally bind, loose, declare, and decree according to the principles in God's Word, we can bring forth "life." The Bible tells us this in Matthew 18:18 (NIV): *"Truly I tell you, whatever you bind on earth will be bound in heaven, and whatever you loose on earth will be loosed in heaven."*

Pray—Especially in Your Heavenly Language (Tongues)

Maintain a good prayer life and stay disciplined. Keep regular communication with God, nurturing and growing your relationship with Him. As important as it is to pray to God in English, it is just as important—if not more important—to pray in tongues. Ephesians 6:18 (NIV) tells us to *"pray in the Spirit on all occasions with all kinds of prayers and requests."*

> If we are praying in tongues, the Holy Spirit is completely controlling our prayers, making them custom-tailored for the situation at hand.

When we pray in tongues, we are praying God's will. Sometimes we are unaware of the spiritual warfare around us. In English, we may not know how to combat properly. If we are praying in tongues, the Holy Spirit is completely controlling our prayers, making them custom-tailored for the situation at hand.

Praying in tongues is one of the gifts of the Spirit and is available to all believers. Acts 2:4 (NIV) says that *"All of them were filled with the Holy Spirit and began to speak in other tongues as the Spirit enabled them."* I believe every Christian can and should be filled with the Holy Spirit. If you are not filled with the Holy Spirit, ask God to fill you. You can receive this gift through the laying on of hands; but God can also give it to you directly, in a moment when you are alone with Him. Ask, and determine in your heart to keep asking until you receive the gift of tongues because you need it!

Once you have the gift, use it. I personally believe that Christians should pray in tongues for a minimum of thirty minutes each day, even if that is while you are in the shower, driving to work, or making dinner. It doesn't matter. Just pray in the Spirit whenever you can because when you do, you are providing God an opportunity to move on your behalf. You are also building yourself up in the Spirit. The Bible tells us this in First Corinthians 14:4 (NIV): *"Anyone who speaks in a tongue edifies themselves."*

Read the Bible

When we maintain a healthy spiritual life, filling ourselves with the truths of God's Word, we create a solid foundation for ourselves to fight off the attacks of the enemy. We will recognize his lies more quickly if we are already filled with the truth. God's Word is alive and more powerful than a two-edged sword (Hebrews 4:12). The Bible is our sword in the Spirit. We need to be using that sword regularly, to offensively fight off the attacks of the enemy.

Take Communion

Taking communion is a way of applying what Jesus did on the cross. It is not necessary to be in church to take communion. You can even take it alone in the comfort of your own home, or anywhere for that matter. The Bible instructs us how to take communion. We are told to examine ourselves and ask for forgiveness. First Corinthians 11:23-32 (ESV) tells us:

> For I received from the Lord what I also delivered to you, that the Lord Jesus on the night when he was betrayed took bread, and when he had given thanks, he broke it, and said, "This is my body, which is for you. Do this in remembrance of me." In the same way also he took the cup, after supper, saying, "This cup is the new covenant in my blood. Do this, as often as you drink it, in remembrance of me." For as often as you eat this bread and drink the cup, you proclaim the Lord's death until he comes.
>
> Whoever, therefore, eats the bread or drinks the cup of the Lord in an unworthy manner will be guilty concerning the body and blood of the Lord. Let a person examine himself, then, and so eat of the bread and drink of the cup. For anyone who eats and drinks without discerning the body eats and drinks judgment on himself. That is why many of you are weak and ill, and some have died. But if we judged ourselves truly, we would not be judged. But when we are judged by the

Lord, we are disciplined so that we may not be condemned along with the world.

Apply Anointing Oil

Use anointing oil to anoint both yourself and your living space regularly. There is nothing special in the actual oil itself. You can use any form of oil, even the olive oil in your kitchen cupboard! Using anointing oil is essentially putting your faith into action. It is a way of showing that you believe in the level of protection and freedom that God has made available to you and that you are choosing to apply it to your life.

> Using anointing oil is essentially putting your faith into action. It is a way of showing that you believe in the level of protection and freedom that God has made available to you and that you are choosing to apply it to your life.

Praise and Worship

Praise and worship are very powerful weapons against the enemy. This goes beyond the praise and worship that happens at church because true praise and worship comes from within us. It is a lifestyle. Make sure you are engaging in personal times of worship regularly. Some of our most powerful times of worship can happen when we are alone with Him. You do not need to know how to sing or play an instrument; just worship

Him in whichever way is right for you. Put on music if need be, but make sure you are taking the time to worship Him often.

Playing anointed worship music within your house regularly—24/7 if possible—is also another way to create an atmosphere of praise and reverence for the Lord. Doing so is a great weapon because oppressive spirits have no desire to be in this kind of godly atmosphere.

Put on the Armor of God

The armor of God is outlined in Ephesians 6:10-17 (NIV):

> *Finally, be strong in the Lord and in his mighty power. Put on the full armor of God, so that you can take your stand against the devil's schemes. For our struggle is not against flesh and blood, but against the rulers, against the authorities, against the powers of this dark world and against the spiritual forces of evil in the heavenly realms. Therefore put on the full armor of God, so that when the day of evil comes, you may be able to stand your ground, and after you have done everything, to stand. Stand firm then, with the belt of truth buckled around your waist, with the breastplate of righteousness in place, and with your feet fitted with the readiness that comes from the gospel of peace. In addition to all this, take up the shield of faith, with which you can*

extinguish all the flaming arrows of the evil one. Take the helmet of salvation and the sword of the Spirit, which is the word of God.

The armor of God is available both as a form of protection and as an offensive weapon against the enemy. It is not of any value to us, however, unless we actively put on this armor. We need to follow what the Bible tells us in Ephesians. Verbally, we must declare that we are putting on the whole armor of God: the helmet of salvation; the breastplate of righteousness; the belt of truth; the shoes of the gospel of peace; the shield of faith; and the sword of the Spirit. Speaking this aloud regularly is one way we can be protected from—and fight against—the spiritual attacks of the enemy.

Ask for Angels

Angels are available to assist Christians, but first they need to receive instruction to do so. Psalm 91:11-12 (NKJV) says, *"He shall give His angels charge over you, to keep you in all your ways. In their hands they shall bear you up, lest you dash your foot against the stone."* We need to ask God to send His angels to protect us. It is important to note that we do not communicate with the angels ourselves. I never talk to the angels directly.

Instead, I ask God to send angels as needed. We do not have the power to command angels to do things, but we can ask God to command them to do things for us that are in accordance with His will. God tells us about this in Hebrews 1:14 (NIV): *"Are not all angels ministering spirits sent to serve those who will inherit salvation?"*

Angels are powerful tools in spiritual warfare, so we must remember to ask God to send them to work on our behalf. It is okay if we do not know what type of angel we need. We can simply pray, asking God to send any angels necessary to help us, protect us, and fight for us to maintain our freedom.

> Angels are powerful tools in spiritual warfare, so we must remember to ask God to send them to work on our behalf.

Use the Name and the Blood of Jesus

It is important for Christians to have a revelation of who they are in Christ and of the authority they carry. The blood of Jesus and the name of Jesus are two very powerful weapons of war that are at our disposal any time we wish to use them. I recommend that you use them often!

The blood of Jesus does so many things for us. One of the things it does is cleanse us. When you feel demonic spirits attacking you, use your mouth to actively plead the blood of Jesus over your body and your mind. This is not complicated. You can say something as simple as, "I plead the blood of Jesus over my body and my mind."

Doing this is such a powerful act because we overcome the enemy by the blood of Jesus (Revelation 12:11).

The blood of Jesus is also a great defensive weapon of war. When we plead the blood of Jesus around ourselves—our homes, vehicles, finances, jobs, ministries, families, pets, relationships, etc.—we are essentially asking for protection from attacks of the enemy. Like the other weapons of warfare, the blood of Jesus needs to be actively applied by faith in order for it to be effective. Once again, we do this by speaking aloud a covering of the blood of Jesus over ourselves, everything pertaining to us, everything we love, and everything over which we have been given stewardship.

I am always pleading the blood of Jesus over everything, especially when I minister, because it is a way of protecting against retaliation and outside spiritual attacks. I even plead the blood of Jesus over my surroundings. Once, during a ministry session, I was pleading the blood of Jesus around the room where I was conducting the session. As I was doing so, the client had a vision of angels pouring the blood of Jesus all over the walls. Her vision was another confirmation to me that the blood of Jesus does indeed protect us when we actively apply it.

There is so much power in the blood of Jesus. Once we have repented, asked for forgiveness, and verbally broken any curses and vows, these sins can then be washed in the blood of Jesus to nullify their effects.

We can do this with a simple prayer such as, "I break any curse of poverty over my life in Jesus' name and command any such curses to be washed in the blood of Jesus."

The name of Jesus works in a similar way. In the name of Jesus, we can break curses, break vows, and command demonic spirits to leave (Mark 16:17-18). There is no other name higher than the name of Jesus. Make sure you activate this powerful weapon by using the name of Jesus aloud frequently.

> There is no other name higher than the name of Jesus. Make sure you activate this powerful weapon by using the name of Jesus aloud frequently.

Overall, it is important for Christians to understand that maintaining freedom following deliverance is active not passive. We are not to be fearful of spirits returning to torment us. We are to be aware of this possibility and informed of how to handle these attacks as they come. Remember, if you have Jesus, that means you have already won the war! Use the tools He has given you and ask Him to help you. If you are faithful to do this, you will successfully walk in freedom.

You can read the following prayer over yourself daily as a form of spiritual warfare:

Pray the Daily Warfare Prayer

Dear heavenly Father,

I repent and ask You to forgive me of my sins. Wash me clean of the effects these sins have had on me. I plead the blood of Jesus over myself, everything pertaining to me, everything I love, and everything I have been given stewardship over. I command any spirits attacking me in any area to leave now in the name of Jesus. I break any curses being spoken or sent against me. I bless anyone who is cursing me, and I render all curses void and command any connected spirits to leave in the name of Jesus.

I repent of all judgments and wash them with the blood of Jesus. I choose to forgive anyone who has wronged or hurt me. I command any spirits connected with any judgments or unforgiveness to leave me now in the name of Jesus. I put on the whole armor of God. Lord, I ask You to release Your ministering angels to me now to assist in removing anything negative. I ask You to protect me and to bless every area of my life. Thank You for allowing me to walk in freedom and for empowering me to fully answer the call You have placed upon my life. In Jesus' name, amen.

CHAPTER 11

WHAT DO I DO NEXT?

My hope is that this book has provided you with a better understanding of the spiritual realm and how it can affect a Christian. If you have not done so already, I would encourage you to go through this book and spend time reading each prayer aloud, giving God the opportunity to minister to you. Freedom and deliverance is a process that you will likely continue to walk out.

ACTIVELY IMPLEMENT THE STRATEGIES...

Remember that you have an active part to play in your own freedom. Just reading about how to live a life that is free from oppression is not enough to make it happen. You must *actively implement the strategies, tools, concepts, and lifestyle changes* necessary to successfully apply what you have learned. Partner with God and ask Him to help you as you take the steps necessary to obtain His freedom both for yourself and for others.

Now may be the time God is asking you to make a lifestyle change. Do you feel like He has liberated you from a spirit that had been causing a sinful behavior? You now need to take all the steps required to discontinue that behavior immediately.

Did God liberate you from a spirit of addiction that had been causing you to drink or smoke? Throw every one of those alcohol bottles and/or cigarettes out right now. Find yourself an accountability partner who will pray with you and assist you in your journey to maintain your freedom from that spirit of addiction.

Did you receive freedom from a spirit of bitterness or unforgiveness? Choose right now to always be quick to forgive those who hurt you, and ask God if there is any person He would have you reach out to and reconcile with.

> Do not be afraid or ashamed to ask for help. That is a trick the devil will use to try and stop you from reaching out to others because he knows that we need each other.

PLUG INTO A LOCAL, SPIRIT-FILLED CHURCH

Plug into a local, Spirit-filled church. When we are properly rooted, not only are we protected but we are also in a position where God can mature us in wisdom, anointings, and giftings. Connect with individuals and leaders who can pray for you and support you on your journey of freedom. Do not be afraid or ashamed to ask for help. That is a trick the devil will use to try and stop you from reaching out to others because he knows that we need each other.

If, after reading this book, you still feel like you are experiencing a spiritual issue, talk to your pastor, leader, or a trusted friend. Ask them to pray for you. Not all churches believe in deliverance ministry or that a Christian can be affected by a demon. In this case, seek the Holy Spirit and ask Him what He would have you do. Some churches do believe in deliverance but are not set up or equipped to deal with deeper spiritual issues. There are many ministries, including the one that I am part of, that offer special deliverance ministry appointments to members of other churches. This type of ministry appointment does not require a person to change churches.

In fact, the ministry I am part of requires a person's pastor to sign a form prior to that person receiving ministry. We want to make sure it is very clear to pastors that we are only offering to assist and not to cause members of their flocks to leave the places God has called them to. There are also many deliverance conferences that a person can attend, where group deliverance ministry is performed.

If your local church is not set up with a deliverance ministry but does believe in it and wants to learn more, there are courses that you or your leaders can take on deliverance ministry—both to receive it and to be equipped to move in it within their own churches. I believe that every church should be equipped to provide deliverance ministry to its own flock. In Appendix C, you will find additional resources outlining how you or your church can receive deliverance ministry and training.

> If you feel God tugging on your heart and you know you are being called to set the captives free, it is important to understand what that requires.

REACH OUT—DELIVERANCE MINISTRY

If you feel God tugging on your heart and you know you are being called to set the captives free, it is important to understand what that requires. Aside from an adequate level of training and spiritual maturity, a deliverance minister must be a person of integrity and love. You must be a person who moves in compassion.

Jesus was a Man of compassion, and He is our perfect example. In the Bible, there are many instances where Jesus had compassion for individuals before He healed them. We need to know how to find God's heart for those we are ministering to so that we too can operate out of a place of love and compassion.

I believe a deliverance minister must also be a person of discretion. During times of ministry, it is not unusual for clients to share their deepest, darkest secrets—often things they have never told anyone before. As a minister, it is beneficial for you to have clients reveal this type of information, as it will assist you in ministering to them. I have noticed that when clients are comfortable and feel you are a trustworthy person, they will open up to you. If you share confidential information with others, however, clients will feel betrayed and you will lose their trust—and possibly your reputation.

Deliverance ministers also need to live lives that are free from sin and open doors. We all sin, yes, but sin needs to be quickly repented of and washed in the blood of Jesus. Satan does not like it when we raid his camp. If he can find an opening where he can attack us, he will. By keeping doors closed and fully consecrating our lives to Jesus, we can minister with a safer level of protection from the enemy and any of his retaliation.

Deliverance ministers also need to be deeply rooted in the Word and possess an adequate level of spiritual maturity. They need to know how to properly pray and do spiritual warfare, thereby keeping themselves protected from any transference of spirits or any retaliation from doing ministry.

I must warn again that deliverance ministry is not to be taken lightly. Individuals should not engage in any form of deliverance ministry without proper training and covering, simply out of concern for the safety of themselves and those receiving ministry. The level of spiritual warfare that surrounds deliverance ministry can be extremely intense. Retaliation can be damaging if you are not properly equipped or set up to handle it. Again, if you do wish to be trained in administering deliverance or wish to establish a deliverance ministry within your church, Appendix C informs you how to proceed.

WALK IT OUT

Now it is time to walk it out! Apply the warfare tools to your life beginning today so that you can maintain your freedom. If this book has impacted you, I encourage you to pass it along. Recommend it to your friends and church family. Knowledge is power, and as Christians we have a mandate to help others walk in freedom as well.

Remember, you are a child of the most high King! He who lives inside you is greater than any oppression you may face. God loves you so much. He wants you to be free, stay free, and live free, because whom the Son sets free is free indeed (John 8:36). I pray that you walk in the high call and destiny that God has for you, living in His freedom every single day!

SALVATION AND DELIVERANCE PRAYERS

SALVATION PRAYER

Do you have a personal relationship with Jesus Christ?

Do you know that it is His desire to spend eternity with you?

Regardless of what you've done or where you are, God wants so deeply to be part of your life. His forgiving power can wash away any sins you've committed. His love can heal any wounds you've experienced. If you haven't already done so, I invite you now to accept Jesus Christ as your Lord and Savior. If you are ready to commit your life to Jesus and follow Him, pray the following prayer aloud:

> *Lord, I confess that I have sinned. I am sorry, and I ask for Your forgiveness. I believe that You sent Your Son, Jesus, to die on the cross. I believe that*

He rose again and that all who accept Him into their hearts can spend eternity with You.

Jesus, I believe that You are the Son of God. Thank You for dying on the cross for me. I confess You as my Lord and Savior. I invite You into my heart and into my life. From this moment forward, I want to live for You. Thank You for empowering me and helping me to live the life You have destined for me. I love You, Lord! Amen.

If you prayed that simple prayer aloud for the first time—congratulations! Having Him as the center of your life will change everything. It is very important to now find a local, Spirit-filled church to attend so that you can connect with other Christians while growing in your relationship with the Lord. Also get a Bible and begin to read the Word.

God bless you as you begin your new journey with Him!

DELIVERANCE PRAYERS

So if the Son sets you free, you will be free indeed (John 8:36 NIV).

Forgiveness Prayer

Lord, I have unforgiveness in my heart. I confess that I have not always loved others. I have harbored resentment and bitterness, but I am coming

to You now to ask You to help me forgive those
who have hurt me. I want to forgive them from
my heart. I don't know if I can, but I make the
choice to do so. Help me to forgive them. Please
take away the pain, the hurt, the resentment,
and the bitterness. Lord, show me now the people
I need to forgive, so I can release them and be
released myself.

Pause, and let the Holy Spirit show you the names or faces of people you need to forgive. They may be living or dead. Take your time; and as the Lord shows them to you, forgive them in your own words. If God shows you individuals you feel you have already forgiven, forgive them again anyway. If God is bringing them to your memory, it is likely because you may still need to forgive them.

Breaking Generational Curses Prayer

Dear heavenly Father,
I confess that I and my generations have sinned
against You. I am sorry for these sins and on
behalf of me and my generations, I repent and
ask for Your forgiveness. (You can list and repent of any specific sins that you know of in your family line, if you wish. Examples of sins include anger, bitterness, lust, adultery, misappropriation of finances, poverty, early death, disease,

addictions, fear, anxiety, lethargy, false idol worship, false religion, depression, mental illness, etc.) *In the name of Jesus, I ask You to please cleanse me in Your blood to remove the effects that these sins and iniquities have had on me and my generational line. I command any connected and related spirits to leave me now in the name of Jesus. I plead the blood of Jesus over me and all of my remaining family line. Amen.*

Breaking Soul Ties Prayer

Dear heavenly Father,

I repent for any ungodly soul ties that I may have created or participated in, whether knowingly or unknowingly. I ask You to please forgive me. In the name of Jesus, I now break and renounce all evil soul ties that I or my generations have had. These include any ungodly soul ties with the Masonic Lodge or any of its orders, ungodly scout or guide organizations, cults or covens, partners I became sexually involved with outside of marriage, partners with which I participated in any ungodly sexual, perverted, or lustful acts, anyone who has ever abused or controlled me in any way, blood buddies, tattoo artists, homosexual or lesbian partners or friends, all close friends and family members (both in my natural family and my spiritual family), spouse, ex-spouse(s), parents, grandparents, great-grandparents, and children. In the name of Jesus, I also break and renounce any evil soul ties with any objects that I may have in my possession. I ask You, God, to show me if I need to get rid of anything that has an ungodly soul tie attached to it. I renounce these and any other evil or ungodly soul ties. I break them and wash them now in the blood of Jesus. Amen.

Breaking Witchcraft Curses Prayer

Dear heavenly Father,

I repent for any involvement that I or my generations had in any form of witchcraft. I ask You to please forgive me and my generations of these sins and to wash them with the blood of Jesus. I renounce every covenant, pact, or agreement that I or my generations made with any psychic, occult contact, cult, false religion, false doctrine, satanist, or with satan himself. In the name of Jesus, I break all demonic holds on me in these areas all the way back to Adam and Eve and wash them with the blood of Jesus. In the name of Jesus, I also break any witchcraft curses that have been spoken or sent against me. I cover myself in the blood of Jesus and command all connected and related spirits to leave me. I bless anyone who has ever cursed me. I claim freedom from those curses and their effects now in the name of Jesus. Amen.

Repentance Prayer

Dear heavenly Father,
I confess that I have sinned, and I repent. I am
sorry for my sins. I ask You to please forgive me
now and to wash me in Your blood. I also confess
that my generations have sinned against You, and
I repent on behalf of them. I ask You to please for-
give them and to wash their sins with the blood of
Jesus. I now break any hold that these sins have
had on me. I break all resulting and connected
curses and spirits and command them to leave me
now in the name of Jesus. Amen.

Take a moment and ask the Holy Spirit if there are
any specific sins that you need to confess and repent of.
In your own words, do so now.

Judgments Prayer

Dear heavenly Father,
I confess that I have judged others, and I realize
that judging is a sin. I repent for doing so. I ask
You to please forgive me for all the judgments I
have made, including those toward family mem-
bers, friends, spiritual leaders, and political
leaders. Please bless all the people I have ever
judged. In the name of Jesus, I break those judg-
ments and all curses involved. I command any

connected demonic spirits to leave in the name of Jesus. Amen.

Leviathan Prayer

Dear heavenly Father,
I repent of my sins and the sins of my ancestors all the way back to Adam and Eve who allowed the spirit of Leviathan to come and torment me. I am sorry for these sins, and I ask You to please forgive me and wash me in Your blood. In the name of Jesus, I break any curses that may have resulted from these sins and cover them with the blood of Jesus. I command any spirits of Leviathan that may be attacking me as a result of such sins or curses to leave me now in the name of Jesus. Amen.

Parent's Prayer Over Child

Dear heavenly Father,
Thank You for _____ (name of child) *and for giving me the honor of being his/her parent. I come to You on behalf of my child and ask You to deliver this precious child of Yours. I repent for any generational sins that may be affecting my child* (name specific sins if you wish), *and I command any connected or related curses to be broken in the name of Jesus. I command any connected or related spirits to leave my child now in the name*

of Jesus. I command any other spirits affecting my child, regardless of the source, to leave him/her now in the name of Jesus (name specific spirits if you wish). *I plead the blood of Jesus over my child, and command everything that is not of God to lift and leave him/her now in the name of Jesus. God, I ask You to please fill my child with spirits of peace and joy, and to bring my child any healing that he/she may need. Thank You, Lord, for setting my child, Your child, free. Amen.*

This prayer, or similar ones, can be prayed over children of any age. As children get older, however, it is important to teach them how to pray for themselves and how to call on God for their own freedom.

Child's Prayer (10 & younger)

Dear Jesus,

I love You, and I am sorry for all the bad things I have done. Please forgive me. I belong to You, and I want to live for You. I forgive everyone who has hurt me, made me mad, or made me cry. I cover myself with the blood of Jesus. I put on the armor of God. The Holy Spirit leads and guides me and helps me know right from wrong. Satan has no control over me.

God, I ask You, in the name of Jesus, to remove the things that hurt me or cause me to do wrong.

God, I also ask You to remove these things from my bedroom and my house, and to send angels to surround me and protect me from the things that want to bother me. God, please help me in every area of my life and take care of me and my family everywhere we go. In Jesus' name, amen.

Child's Prayer (11 & older)

Dear Jesus,

I love You, and I repent for all the bad things I have done. Please forgive me and cleanse me in Your blood. I belong to You and I want to live for You. I choose to break all ties with satan and to close any access points that I may have opened to him. I forgive everyone who has hurt me or wronged me. I bless them, and I ask You to take all of the hurt and pain away. I cover myself with the blood of Jesus. I put on the armor of God. I ask for angels to protect and surround me everywhere I go. The Holy Spirit leads me, guides me, and helps me know right from wrong. Satan is not in control of me—in Jesus I have all authority over him and his demons.

God, I ask You, in the name of Jesus, to remove the things that hurt me or cause me to do wrong. I command anything that is not of God to leave me now in the name of Jesus. I also ask You, God, to remove any bad spirits from my bedroom and my house. If there is any object that I own that I need to get rid of, I ask You to show me and to help me get rid of it. God, I ask You to protect me from the things that want to bother me. God, please help me and bless me in every area of my life. Help me to learn, grow, and prosper in the things of You. Please take care of me and my family everywhere we go and help us serve You all the days of our lives. In Jesus' name, amen.

House Cleansing Prayer

Dear heavenly Father,

Thank You for cleansing me and my home in the blood of Jesus. I ask You to send Your angels into this place to sweep through and remove anything residing here that is not of You. In Jesus' name, I command any demonic spirits that are taking up residence in the foundation, walls, furnishings, or anywhere else in my home to leave now.

I command any demonic spirits that were trans-ferred, have been sent on assignment, came in with any person, or entered through sin, includ-ing through any song, TV show, or movie, to leave this place now in the name of Jesus. (You can also list any specific spirits that you feel are in your home if you wish, commanding them out in the name of Jesus.) *I take authority over the space You have given me. I thank You, God, for sending*

Your angels to cleanse it with the precious blood of Jesus. I also ask, God, that You post angels throughout this home and around the property, to protect against any future demonic intrusions. Amen.

Objects With Demonic Spirits Prayer

Dear heavenly Father,
Thank You, Lord, for caring about my freedom. I ask for Your Holy Spirit to fill this place. Please show me if there are any objects within my home or among my possessions that have demonic spirits attached to them. Please also reveal what You would have me do with these objects and supernaturally empower me to obey Your direction without hesitation. I ask this now in the name of Jesus. Amen.

Pause and allow the Holy Spirit to show you any objects with spirits attached, along with the action He would have you take. Once He shows you, act immediately before the enemy attacks with contradicting thoughts.

Daily Warfare Prayer

Dear heavenly Father,
I repent and ask You to forgive me of my sins. Wash me clean of the effects these sins have had

on me. I plead the blood of Jesus over myself, everything pertaining to me, everything I love, and everything I have been given stewardship over. I command any spirits attacking me in any area to leave now in the name of Jesus. I break any curses being spoken or sent against me. I bless anyone who is cursing me, and I render all curses void and command any connected spirits to leave in the name of Jesus.

I repent of all judgments and wash them with the blood of Jesus. I choose to forgive anyone who has wronged or hurt me. I command any spirits connected with any judgments or unforgiveness to leave me now in the name of Jesus. I put on the whole armor of God. Lord, I ask You to release Your ministering angels to me now to assist in removing anything negative. I ask You to protect me and to bless every area of my life. Thank You for allowing me to walk in freedom and for empowering me to fully answer the call You have placed upon my life. In Jesus' name, amen.

HOW TO MAINTAIN YOUR FREEDOM SUMMARY

You can maintain your freedom by using your weapons of spiritual warfare:

- Fully consecrate your life to Christ.
- Confess your sins and repent.
- Forgiveness.
- Attend church and maintain proper spiritual alignment.
- Bind and loose, declare and decree.
- Pray—especially in your heavenly language (tongues).
- Read the Bible.
- Take Communion.
- Apply anointing oil.
- Praise and worship.

- Put on the armor of God.
- Ask for angels.
- Use the name and the blood of Jesus.
- Pray the daily warfare prayer.

DELIVERANCE RESOURCES

For additional copies of this book, personal deliverance ministry, equipping and empowering for your church and leaders, or group/congregation deliverance ministry, please contact Joanna Adams at Eagle Worldwide Ministries: www.eagleworldwide.com.

The Spirit of the Lord God is upon me, because the Lord has anointed me to bring good news to the poor; he has sent me to bind up the brokenhearted, to proclaim liberty to the captives, and the opening of the prison to those who are bound (Isaiah 61:1 ESV).

ABOUT JOANNA ADAMS

Joanna Adams is a graduate of the Brownsville Revival School of Ministry. As the deliverance director at Eagle Worldwide Ministries, she has a heart to see the captives set free. Joanna has firsthand experience helping Christians receive freedom through personal deliverance ministry. She leads freedom and healing conferences worldwide.

Joanna is also a round table member of the International Society of Deliverance Ministers. Joanna and her husband, Derek, are the senior pastors of Eagles' Nest Fellowship in Ancaster, Ontario, Canada. They travel internationally, bringing freedom to the oppressed, healing to the sick, and prophetic words to the body of Christ.

Joanna is grateful for God's precious gift, her wonderful son, Malachi.

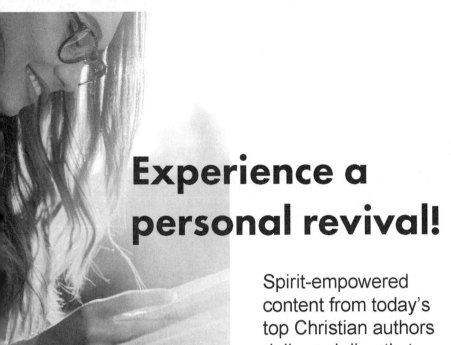

PRISON BOOK PROJECT
P.O. BOX 1146
Sharpes, FL 32959